£0.75p.

67744

THE LAST DAYS OF STEAM ON THE
EASTERN REGION

B1 class no. 61097 of New England depot heading north with a long train of coal empties.

THE LAST DAYS OF STEAM ON THE
EASTERN REGION

– ERIC SAWFORD –

SUTTON PUBLISHING

First published in 1999 by
Sutton Publishing Limited . Phoenix Mill
Thrupp . Stroud . Gloucestershire . GL5 2BU

British Library Cataloguing-in-Publication Data.

A catalogue record for this book is available from the British Library.

ISBN 0-7509-1616-8

Title page photograph: One of Sir Nigel Gresley's most successful designs was the V2 class 2–6–2, introduced in 1936. Officially classified 6MT, these powerful engines were capable of handling the heaviest express trains. Indeed during the war they performed many herculean haulage tasks. Prototype engine no. 60800 *Green Arrow* is seen here at Huntingdon. This was a King's Cross engine and was more often seen on passenger workings.

29.7.52

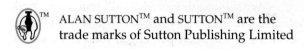
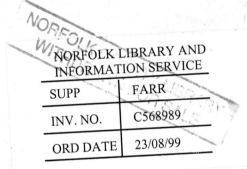

™ ALAN SUTTON™ and SUTTON™ are the trade marks of Sutton Publishing Limited

Typeset in 10/12 Palatino.
Typesetting and origination by
Sutton Publishing Limited.
Printed in Great Britain by
Butler & Tanner, Frome, Somerset.

Introduction

Steam on the Eastern Region was to see its 'swansong' during the 1950s. Only a few diesel locomotives were then in service, and those that were, at that time, were mostly shunting locomotives. Towards the end of the decade many changes took place, and motive power reorganization from 1956 onwards resulted in inter-regional changes. By this time the writing was already on the wall for steam power as diesel locomotives and multiple units were entering service at an ever-increasing rate.

This book looks at the Eastern Region as it was in the early years of the 1950s. At this time there were ten Motive Power Districts, allocated codes 30 to 40 inclusive. By far the largest depot was Stratford, shedcode 30A, with over 400 locomotives in its allocation. The five sheds within its control, Hertford East, Bishops Stortford, Southend Victoria, Colchester and Parkeston, had a further 140 engines.

Stratford in steam days was a fascinating place, always busy, with seemingly endless engine movements taking place. In the mid-1950s 'Britannias' were the principal passenger engines with 'Sandringhams', B1s and B12s still there in considerable numbers. For many visitors the numerous ex-Great Eastern engines were the main attraction, while 0–6–0Ts, a few 2–4–2Ts and 0–6–0s of classes J15, J17, J19 and J20 were always present. In addition, there was the nearby locomotive works, not just for those ex-works but for veterans having made their last journey; at this time these included E4 2–4–0s and examples of the J70 tram engines. Some of the shunting work was still being done by the sturdy Y4 class 0–4–0Ts introduced by A.J. Hill in 1913.

The adjoining district of Cambridge consisted of five depots, with Cambridge itself (31A) having an allocation not far short of 100 engines, and they were a fascinating selection at this time. In the mid-1950s this was one place where you could be certain of seeing a 2–4–0 tender locomotive in action, the last survivors of the ex-Midland South Western Junction Railway 2–4–0s on the Western Region having been withdrawn. Many of the remaining E4s were based at Cambridge, although Norwich still had seven and Lowestoft one at this time. Numerous enthusiasts travelled to Cambridge to see and record on film the E4s at work. Their duties still included passenger, local light goods and station pilot work. Usually one or two were to be seen stored in the shed yard as there were still spare engines available. Also present was a stud of well-maintained J15 class 0–6–0s. Probably their most demanding duty was the first out and last return train on the Kettering service, on so many occasions worked by no. 65390. Examples of the class were also regulars on the Mildenhall and Colne Valley services.

One design which sadly has no example in preservation is the 'Claud' D16 class 4–4–0s which were a mainstay of East Anglian services for many years. Cambridge had a sizeable stud in the mid-1950s, and among their duties was one which took them to Bletchley. No. 62585 was frequently used on this turn, looking strangely out of place among the LMS designs on Bletchley shed while it was serviced before the return working.

Three class G5 0–4–4Ts of North Eastern Railway origin were transferred to work the Bartlow branch; all were officially on 31A's books and one was often to be seen standing in the shed yard. The last remaining class F6 2–4–2Ts saw little work in their final years. Other designs in the Cambridge allocation were 'Sandringhams', B1s, J17s, J19s and J20s. Always in immaculate condition was B2 class no. 61671 *Royal Sovereign*, the Royal engine, and its reserve, no. 61617 *Ford Castle*.

The largest shed in the district was March (31B) with approximately 160 locomotives. This was principally a freight engine depot, servicing the busy Whitemoor marshalling yards nearby. The remaining three sheds were King's Lynn, South Lynn and Bury St Edmunds, none of which had a particularly large number of engines on its books. King's Lynn was the largest with nearly forty, several of which were 'Clauds', D16 4–4–0s, used on local passenger duties.

Norwich, shedcode 32A, was head of a district that had depots along the Norfolk/Suffolk coast. Norwich had over 100 locomotives, many of them passenger types working services to Liverpool Street and elsewhere. At this time these were B1 class 4–6–0s and the 'Britannias', the latter doing so much to improve services on this line right from their introduction in 1951. The other depots were three in Yarmouth, South Town, Vauxhall and the M&GN line, Yarmouth Beach and one at Melton Constable.

The three depots in the 33 district, Plaistow, Tilbury and Shoeburyness, were all under London Midland Region control until they were transferred in 1949, but all three were closed in 1962. As might be expected, most of the locomotives were former LMS designs, with a considerable number of Standard class 4MT 2–6–4Ts having been drafted in in the early 1950s.

The East Coast main line was of particular interest to many enthusiasts. Here were to be found the express passenger locomotives designed by Sir Nigel Gresley; the principal shed, King's Cross (34A), widely known as 'Top Shed', had a considerable number of 'Pacifics' and no fewer than nineteen A4s. The total allocation in the mid-1950s was 133. This figure included L1 2–6–4Ts, elderly ex-Great Northern J52s, 0–6–0STs and fifty-seven N2 class 0–6–2Ts; the latter were responsible for suburban workings. There were four other sheds within the King's Cross district. Hornsey was home to a considerable number of shunting engines in the London area, the remainder of the depot's sixty-plus allocation being J6 class 0–6–0s and N2 0–6–2Ts. Just a few miles further north was Hatfield, whose depot was in a cramped area to the western side of the main line. This was a small shed with almost thirty locomotives, all tank designs. Hitchin had around the same number, including eight B1 class 4–6–0s; at this time these were mainly used on outer suburban services. There were also two ex-Great Eastern veterans there for part of the 1950s: J15 0–6–0 no. 65479 and E4 2–4–0 no. 62785; these were principally used for working the RAF Henlow leave trains. The J15 was, on rare occasions, also used to work trains to Connington tip. The last shed was Neasden (34E) on the Great Central line. In the early 1950s seven A3 class 'Pacifics' were to be found here as well as L1 2–6–4Ts, B1s, N5 shunting tanks and three of the remaining C13 class 4–4–2Ts, a Great Central design introduced in 1903. Strangest of all were two Great Western engines, class 14xx 0–4–2T no. 1473 and class 54xx no. 5409. In 1958 Neasden was transferred to the London Midland Region, becoming part of the Cricklewood district with shedcode 14D.

Peterborough has always been an important railway junction, and in the 1950s there were more lines radiating out from it than there are now. The principal shed of this

The class J2 locomotives were introduced by the Great Northern Railway just one year after the very similar J6 design first appeared. The J2s were fitted with 5ft 8in driving wheels, as opposed to the 5ft 2in of the more numerous J6s. In British Railways days these engines received the 2MT power classification. No. 65023, fresh from its last general overhaul, is seen here at Lincoln on a running-in turn before going back to its home shed, Colwick. It was withdrawn from service in November 1953.

26.8.51

district was New England, one of the largest Eastern Region depots with 168 locomotives in 1954. Many of the duties were heavy freight to Ferme Park, London, worked by WD 2–8–0s and Standard 9F 2–10–0s. New England engines also regularly worked to Colwick and York. In addition a large number of ex-Great Northern J6 class 0–6–0s were allocated here; these were mainly used for shunting at the many brickworks in the area, short trip workings and engineers' trains.

In the 1950s Peterborough North station still retained the overall roof. The track curved through the station and express trains sometimes had difficulty in restarting, especially in wet, greasy conditions. New England had a stud of ex-Great Northern C12 class 4–4–2Ts; their duties included banking northbound expresses and empty stock working. I can well recall these engines with their sharp exhaust note blasting through the station on banking duty. Other members of the class were used on branch lines in the area. With so much heavy freight passing through Peterborough there were extensive sidings where J52 class 0–6–0STs were to be seen on shunting work.

The former Midland shed at Peterborough Spital Bridge was transferred to the Eastern Region in 1950, becoming shedcode 35C. During the following ten years until closure in 1960 it retained a considerable number of locomotives of LMS origin. In the final years D16 class 4–4–0s and B1 class 4–6–0s used on cross-country services were allocated here, with a small number of J39 class 0–6–0s used on freight work.

During the 1950s many local passenger services in East Anglia were worked by 'Claud Hamilton' class 4–4–0s, officially classed D16. No. 62551 is seen at St Ives with the afternoon King's Lynn–Cambridge service. Note the white discs (as opposed to lamps) in use at the time. All traces of the railway at this location have long since disappeared.

8.2.51

Grantham shed was at its most interesting during the mid-1950s, mainly because of its 'Pacifics'; these were A3s and Peppercorn A1s plus a solitary A2, no. 60533 *Happy Knight*. Later in the 1950s the A1s moved away and were replaced by A3s and two more A2s. Grantham was also home to eight B12 4–6–0s in the mid-1950s; these were used principally on local passenger work. Iron ore workings in the area resulted in a stud of O2 class 2–8–0s being on the depot's books. It was not a large shed with around fifty engines, the balance being made up of shunting locomotives and three J6 class 0–6–0s, plus the usual allocation of two A5 class 4–6–2Ts.

The final shed on the East Coast main line was Doncaster (36A), a sizeable depot with more than 170 locomotives and three other depots within its district. During the 1950s Doncaster was a very interesting shed to visit, not just for its own allocation but for what might be there visiting, or ex-works. Among these, on many occasions, were Scottish Region 'Pacifics'. Included among the depot's own engines in the mid-1950s was the streamlined W1 class 4–6–4 no. 60700, which was regularly used on a London turn; the sole Eastern Region Beyer-Garratt 2–8–8–2T no. 69999; five S1 class 0–8–4Ts built for hump shunting; A3 'Pacifics', K3s, V2s, B1s and a variety of 0–6–0s of Great Northern,

Great Central and LNER origin; there were also a considerable number of shunting tanks and WD class 2–8–0s, which were used on coal workings in the area. Frodingham (36C), Barnsley (36D) and Retford (36E), the latter consisting of the GN and GC sheds, all had sizeable numbers of freight engines of 2–8–0 and 0–6–0 wheel arrangements; they were also responsible for a considerable number of shunting locomotives between them.

The 37 district consisted of three depots, all of Great Northern Railway origin. Ardsley (37A) was the principal shed with nearly 100 engines, a small number being used for passenger work. Copley Hill (Leeds), 37B, was very different with around forty locomotives; these consisted of a large number of express engines of classes A1 and A3, together with a few V2 and B1s. It was also home in the mid-1950s to fifteen N1 class 0–6–2Ts. The third shed was Bradford, again with forty-plus engines. The largest mixed traffic engines were B1 class 4–6–0s, the remainder consisting of 0–6–0 and shunting locomotives.

The second largest of the Eastern Region depots was to be found at Colwick (Nottingham), principal shed of the 38 district. Colwick itself was originally a Great Northern Railway depot. In the mid-1950s, over 200 engines were to be found there, among them a sizeable stud of 04s and WD 2–8–0s, the surrounding collieries generating most of the work for these engines. It was also home to a large number of K2 and K3 class 2–6–0s. Of particular interest in the mid-1950s were the J5 class, shortly to become extinct. These were an Ivatt design introduced by the Great Northern in 1909. The shunting engines were a mixture of GN and GC designs.

All four depots – Annesley, Leicester (GC), Staveley (GC) and Woodford Halse – which came within Colwick's control were ex-Great Central sheds. All except Leicester were home to principally goods engines of 2–8–0 and 0–6–0 wheel arrangement. Leicester was a comparatively small shed, with just twenty-four engines including five A3 'Pacifics', three V2 class 2–6–2s and over a dozen B1s, all of which were used on Great Central passenger services. In 1958 Annesley, Leicester and Woodford Halse were transferred to the London Midland Region, Colwick following eight years later.

The two depots that comprised the 39 district, Gorton and Sheffield (Darnall), were originally Great Central Railway sheds. Both were large, Gorton having more than 170 engines and Sheffield about 110. During the mid-1950s many of the locomotives were of GC origin, the others being mostly LNER designs. At Gorton locomotives awaiting entry into, or fresh from, the nearby locomotive works could be seen.

The final district was controlled by Lincoln (40A) with five other depots, varying considerably in size, under its control. Lincoln was home to seventy-five engines with a large number being 0–6–0s of GC and LNER origin; among its subsheds was Lincoln St Marks. In the 1950s D11 'Director' class 4–4–0s were employed on cross-country services, among them the sole survivor no. 62660 *Butler-Henderson*. The shunting locomotives were mostly ex-Great Eastern J69 class 0–6–0Ts; this is not surprising as the LNER spread examples of this class far and wide, even up to the Scottish sheds.

Immingham (40B) was much larger than Lincoln, with 130 locomotives of a wide range of designs. They included a stud of B1 4–6–0s which were kept in immaculate condition, their primary duty being the King's Cross service, and you could be sure that the B1s on this duty would appear in first-class condition. The Up train ran from Peterborough to London non-stop, the return service making its first stop at Huntingdon. On the main line both trains had a fast timing. B1s from the depot were also seen on fish trains to London. When the 'Britannias' were displaced by diesels in East Anglia, several were sent to Immingham and these took over the service to London for a short time before diesel power on the main line replaced them in turn. They were, however, to see further service on the London Midland Region.

Crowds of youngsters crowd round A1 class no. 60141 *Abbotsford* as it stands at King's Cross ready to leave with a late afternoon train to Leeds. Photography at King's Cross was particularly difficult in the early 1960s owing to the number of people present. Diesels had already replaced steam on some workings.

8.61

Of the four other sheds Louth (40C) was the smallest with just four engines. Tuxford (40D) was not much larger with seventeen in the mid-1950s, all 0–6–0s. Langwith Junction (40E) had sixty and Boston (40F) nearly forty. Langwith was home to a considerable number of heavy goods engines of the 2–8–0 wheel arrangement. Boston had an allocation of twelve K2 class 2–6–0s and eight J69 0–6–0Ts used for dock and general shunting, together with two N5 class 0–6–2Ts. The largest tank locomotives present were four A5 class 4–6–2Ts.

Unfortunately, the Eastern Region refused to issue permits to individuals to visit locomotive depots. The only way that you could be sure of getting round the sheds was to join one of the many organized parties that were commonplace in the 1950s. These were usually marathons, often involving starting out late on a Saturday, arriving at the start point early on Sunday morning, and frequently having to wait until the coach arrived. The tour leader would have done his homework in advance as far as the route, depots and timings were concerned, but life was not easy for the coach driver who sometimes found access difficult; the strange locations and finding the sheds quite often caused problems. In those days a very useful booklet giving directions was available, but it was written

During the early 1960s there were withdrawn locomotives lying in the yards in many Eastern Region depots awaiting their final journey to the scrapyard. Quite often parts were removed to keep others in service. The four engines shown here, J20 no. 64699, J17 no. 65582, and K3s nos 61915 and 61942, stood at March for a considerable time before they were scrapped. March depot was better than most in that the chimneys of stored engines were covered with old tarpaulin. Most engines withdrawn in the 1960s ended up in private scrapyards.

26.5.63.

basically for individuals. On arrival, the tour leader would present the permit at the shedmaster's office. Most participants were only interested in numbers, and the speed that they could get round a shed was unbelievable! Anyone interested in photography usually only had time to go round the shed yard. The speed merchants would soon be back on the coach and ready for the off! These tours usually had an itinerary of around ten depots, but often additional visits would be included; in many cases access was gained even though no permit had been issued. Most tours ended around 5 or 6 p.m., usually at a different station from where the tour started. Tired and dirty after a long but enjoyable day, it was time for the journey home. Those were the days!

Fortunately the Eastern Region would grant lineside permits for photography, subject to seeing a sample of work produced and the signing of an indemnity. For a number of years I was granted this facility which enabled me to record on film a considerable number of locomotives and trains on the East Coast main line and also cross-country routes.

Three examples of the A2 class were allocated to New England depot and were regularly used on semi-fasts to King's Cross in the early 1950s. Their duties also included the first local passenger train to King's Cross on Sundays. No. 60505 *Thane of Fife* was on this duty when it was photographed leaving Huntingdon amid clouds of steam. Note the rather austere straight-sided chimney with a small rim fitted to these engines at this time.

11.7.54

At the start of the 1950s numerous types of pre-grouping locomotive were still in service, with several classes represented only by a few examples. Other designs that had not been particularly successful were to be quickly withdrawn at the start of the decade. One class long familiar on the East Coast main line disappeared at this time: the famous Ivatt 'Atlantic' C1 4–4–2s. The last survivor was withdrawn on arrival at Doncaster with a commemorative special. The 1950s was a period of change: new locomotives of LNER design had already arrived on the scene. With the arrival of the first 'Standards' in 1951 one area which was to change quickly with the arrival of the 'Britannias' was the East Anglian service between London and Norwich.

The East Coast main line was not short of motive power for passenger work, but there was a lack of heavy goods locomotives. The first 'Standards' to be seen south of Peterborough were in fact 9F 2–10–0s, and after initial teething problems, those allocated to New England soon proved themselves, becoming a familiar sight working heavy coal trains to Ferme Park, London, and elsewhere.

During the 1950s I photographed D16/3 class no. 62618, one of the two Royal 'Clauds', on many occasions, but only once with the engine resplendent in LNER green livery. This picture was taken at St Ives on the King's Lynn–Cambridge service. The engine was repainted in October 1949, creating considerable interest, but this livery was comparatively short-lived and the engine reverted to the standard lined black livery in October 1952. It remained in service until November 1959.

30.1.51

The express services remained firmly in the hands of Gresley and Peppercorn 'Pacifics', backed by the true 'maids of all work', the V2 class 2–6–2s. 'Britannias' were only to be seen regularly, albeit for a short time, on the King's Cross–Immingham services in the early 1960s, having been displaced by diesels in East Anglia. Within a short time this was to happen again as diesel power replaced steam on the main and secondary lines.

On the Great Central, express services were in the hands of A3 'Pacifics' and B1s, the final years seeing Stanier class 5s heading most trains. On the former Great Eastern lines the 'Britannias' remained the principal express motive power, B1 class 4–6–0s also handling many services. In the mid-1950s it seemed that steam power would be the norm for many more years, and certainly the cross-country and branch lines were firmly in the hands of steam. How quickly all this was to change with the rapid influx of diesel multiple units and diesel locomotives for main line and shunting work.

Early in the 1960s things were very different, and steam was still commonplace on the main line. The King's Cross engines in particular were in fine mechanical and external condition. Within a short time diesels were to be seen on principal expresses. The non-stop London–Edinburgh service, 'The Elizabethan', was steam-hauled by King's Cross and Haymarket engines up to the end of 1962. King's Cross depot closed in June 1963, the few remaining serviceable locomotives being transferred to New England and Grantham. Such was the speed of change that the site was almost completely cleared in

Visitors to Doncaster depot at weekends would normally find one or more Pacifics, fresh from overhaul in the works. They often included engines from north of the border, such as A3 no. 60037 *Hyperion* of Haymarket shed, Edinburgh. Visiting enthusiasts from the south always hoped that one of the four Carlisle Canel depot A3s would be present.

24.6.56

the following year. Grantham also closed in 1963 leaving New England to soldier on until January 1965. By this time it had become a shadow of its former self: many tracks were empty, and withdrawn and stored engines were to be seen. The last shed to operate steam on the main line in the region was Doncaster which closed in April 1966.

March was the last depot in East Anglia with steam, losing its allocation in November 1963. By this time the large depot with its distinctive coaling tower, a local landmark in the surrounding Fens, had just a small number of serviceable locomotives. Others had stood in the yard for some considerable time awaiting their final journey. Although officially closed to steam, visitors continued to arrive for some time afterwards, mostly from the London Midland Region. Sundays would find Stanier class 5s and 8Fs present and the occasional Stanier 5MT 2–6–0s alongside an increasing number of diesel locomotives.

Several of the Eastern Region depots were transferred to the London Midland in the late 1950s. Colwick remained until January 1966, by this time consisting of mostly B1s, 04s and WD 2–8–0s. Of the former 39 district Gorton had become part of the LMR in 1958, closing in 1966, while Sheffield Darnell lost its steam locomotives in June 1963. Two other former LMR sheds, Staveley Midland and Canklow, closed in 1965. Langwith Junction, at this time 41J, closed in February 1966 having just three B1 4–6–0s in service, all of which were transferred to departmental use as stationary boilers. Just two months later the last shed on the Eastern Region, Doncaster, closed, its few remaining locomotives making their final journey.

I have lived by the main line for many years and working on this book has brought back countless memories. I have included as many locomotive types as possible from the final years of steam on the Eastern Region, including engines of pre-grouping origin, the London & North Eastern Railway and also a few Standards and LMS designs which were occasionally to be seen. The Eastern Region was fortunate in having some of the finest track in Britain. King's Cross and its famous 'Top Link' drivers and their exploits are well recorded. When the last streamlined A4 left King's Cross on a regular service I for one never thought that one of Sir Nigel Gresley's 'Pacifics' would head north from the capital again. The *Flying Scotsman* was of course to be the first, followed in recent years by *Union of South Africa* and *Sir Nigel Gresley* carrying 'The Elizabethan' and 'The Flying Scotsman' headboards, recalling the great days of steam on this famous route to the north.

Eric Sawford
July 1998

Fortunately six A4 locomotives survived the scrapman's torch, although two of them were to make the long journey across the North Atlantic. No. 60008 *Dwight D. Eisenhower* was one of these, and it is preserved at the National Rail Road Museum, USA. Here the locomotive is seen in immaculate condition at King's Cross heading the 'Yorkshire Pullman'. No. 60008 was withdrawn in July 1963, the month after King's Cross (Top Shed) closed.

9.61

The wheel tapper waits with his hammer and inspection lamp at the ready as A4 no. 60034 *Lord Farringdon* drifts into King's Cross. Although diesels had already taken over many of the principal main line services at this time, the King's Cross A4s were still in immaculate condition. *Lord Farringdon* was to end its working life in Scotland; it was withdrawn from Aberdeen in August 1966, ending its days in a Northumberland scrapyard.

9.61

The N2s were once a familiar sight at King's Cross on suburban and empty stock workings. No. 69560, still with British Railways on the tankside, is seen here on empty stock duties. Many members of the class were fitted with condensing apparatus but this engine, built by Beyer Peacock & Company in 1925, was not. No. 69560 was withdrawn in October 1960.

9.7.53

The summer services were eagerly awaited by enthusiasts as 'The Elizabethan' workings were shared between Edinburgh (Haymarket) and King's Cross engines. No. 60009 *Union of South Africa* was a frequent visitor from north of the border. When this photograph was taken, the coaching stock had already been taken out of the station to enable the engine to be moved for servicing. The *Union of South Africa* has become very well known in preservation.

9.61

Grantham shed's A1 no. 60157 *Great Eastern* passes through Huntingdon with a southbound special. This locomotive was later transferred to King's Cross shed where it remained until 1959, when it moved to Doncaster to end its working life. It was withdrawn from service in January 1965. After a short period in store *Great Eastern* was towed to Draper's of Hull and cut up.

1.8.54

Still with 'The Elizabethan' headboard in place, no. 60009 *Union of South Africa* is coaled at the small locomotive yard adjacent to King's Cross station. This yard has long since gone and the site is currently used for the storage of building materials. During steam days comings and goings could easily be watched from the platform end. Note the emblem on the side of the locomotive.

9.61

While the A4s were kept in immaculate condition it was not the same for many of the A3s. No. 60054 *Prince of Wales* is pictured here in a poor condition: note the burnt patch at the base of the smokebox door. A Grantham engine at this time, it ended its days at New England from where it was withdrawn in July 1964.

9.61

Several L1 class 2–6–4Ts were allocated to Hitchin depot where they were principally used on local passenger duties. No. 67746, pictured here in the shed yard, had been 'stopped' for repairs judging from what appears to be part of the side tank lying on the top of the tankside. This was one of the batch built by the North British Locomotive Company. It entered service in December 1948 and withdrawn in July 1962.

14.10.56

The locomotive shed at Hitchin was situated immediately behind the station building on the eastern side of the main line in rather cramped conditions. The shed's allocation included a number of J6 class 0–6–0s of Great Northern Railway origin. No. 64197 was completed at Doncaster in May 1913 and remained in service until October 1959. The Hitchin J6s were principally employed on local goods and engineers' trains.

14.10.56

Enthusiasts visiting Hitchin shed were often surprised to see E4 2–4–0 no. 62785 in the shed yard. This engine and J15 no. 65479 were transferred there to work the RAF Henlow leave trains over the Bedford branch but the E4 spent much of its time idle in the yard. This engine is the sole survivor of the class and can be seen resplendent in Great Eastern Railway blue livery at Bressingham Steam Museum.

14.10.56

The J15 class no. 65479 was also based at Hitchin to work RAF Henlow leave trains; it worked in company with E4 no. 62785 which can be seen in the background. The J15 was the more useful engine and was frequently used on other duties including trips up the East Coast main line to Connington tip. This shed location is still easily recognizable; most of the track has long since gone but the site has not been put to any other use.

14.10.56

The Cambridge–King's Cross trains were mostly worked by B1s in the mid-1950s, although 'Sandringhams' were not uncommon. No. 61653 *Huddersfield Town* arrives at Hitchin. This was one of the Darlington-built engines, completed in April 1936. When this picture was taken it was a Cambridge engine, but it moved to March the following year, from where it was withdrawn in January 1960, ending its working days at Doncaster Works.

14.10.56

N2 class locomotives were a familiar sight in the London area for many years, mostly on suburban passenger and empty stock workings. They were capable of a fair turn of speed with their 5ft 8in driving wheels. Often heavy northbound expresses leaving London would find an N2 heading a suburban train running parallel, its driver intent on showing a clean pair of heels to the express as its locomotive slowly gained speed. No. 69515 is seen here at Hitchin in company with a J6 and a J15.

14.10.56

The cold crisp conditions of a February morning add to the smoke effect produced by B1 class no. 61097 of New England depot as it heads north with a long train of coal empties. Several examples of this class were among the last engines to be found at New England prior to the depot's closure in January 1965.

28.2.63

The Great Eastern Railway constructed a considerable number of 0–6–0T locomotives of several classes. No. 68638, pictured here in the cramped space of Hitchen shed, was an example of the J68 class introduced by A.J. Hill in 1912. This class was a development of earlier designs with side-window cab. Note the rather battered Westinghouse pump: these were inclined to stick, and were often hit by a coal hammer to free them.

14.10.56

New England depot's allocation included several A2 class locomotives, which were the usual motive power for semi-fast passenger services to London. A2/3 no. 60513 *Dante* is seen here leaving Huntingdon on its way to King's Cross with a train of mixed stock, including a full brake next to the engine. No. 60513 spent several years at New England, being withdrawn from there in February 1963; it was cut up at Doncaster Works three months later.

9.5.54

This is one of those rare moments that occasionally occur in railway photography: the prototype A2 no. 60500 *Edward Thompson* and the first V2 no. 60800 *Green Arrow* stand side by side at Huntingdon. The A2 was working the afternoon King's Cross–Peterborough service while *Green Arrow* was in charge of a pick-up goods. The A2s' unattractive straight-sided chimney was later replaced with one of the more suitable lipped type.

29.7.52

B1 no. 61210 attacks the 1-in-200 climb from Huntingdon to Abbots Ripton in fine style at the head of a mixed goods. These powerful mixed traffic 4–6–0s were to be found in the Eastern, North Eastern and Scottish Regions, and 410 examples were built between 1942 and 1951. They were built at Doncaster, Darlington and Gorton, and some were also constructed by the Vulcan Foundry and the North British Locomotive Company. No. 61210 was completed by the latter in July 1947.

6.7.59

The first example of the V2 class emerged from Doncaster Works in June 1936, just one year after the streamlined A4 class had made its debut. The V2s were powerful mixed traffic engines, and they soon proved their capabilities. In all 184 examples were constructed at Doncaster and Darlington Works. The last example, no. 60983, was completed at the latter in July 1944, construction having gone on throughout the war years. No. 60914, a King's Cross engine, is seen here leaving Huntingdon heading a Peterborough semi-fast.

18.6.57

During the 1950s there were a few changes among the A3s that were regularly seen south of Peterborough. Locomotives from the North Eastern and very occasionally the Scottish Region appeared, the latter usually on running-in turns after a visit to Doncaster Works. Here, no. 60062 *Minoru* approaches Huntingdon at speed with a Newcastle express. This locomotive remained in service until December 1964, being withdrawn from New England shed.

26.6.54

This was another lucky photograph: A3 no. 60050 *Persimmon* heading a Peterborough semi-fast waits at Huntingdon as V2 no. 60948 passes on the slow road with a complete train of bolster wagons. Both locomotives were allocated to New England depot. Time was rapidly running out for the A3: it was withdrawn just three months after this photograph was taken. The V2 did not fare much better, being withdrawn in September 1963.

28.3.63

Fast fish trains, usually headed by a B1 or K3 class locomotive, were a daily sight on the East Coast main line in the 1950s. Anyone on the station platform was left in little doubt as to the train's cargo after it had passed through! No. 61392 heads for London having been given the 'Up main' after passing through Huntingdon station.

12.9.54

No. 60017 *Silver Fox* hauling a relief express runs past the two sets of signals which were to be found just to the south of Huntingdon station. These signals enabled trains to be turned slow road or from the slow to the main line. The two posts, no longer in use when this photograph was taken, at one time enabled trains to run into Huntingdon East station. During the war, ambulance trains were run into this station for unloading on several occasions. After the war there was no reason to retain the connection, and the line was taken out, although the signal posts remained there for many years as a reminder.

1.8.54

Prior to the arrival of Standard 9F 2–10–0s at New England most goods trains were handled by WD 2–8–0s. Here, no. 90191 heads north near Huntingdon no. 2 signal box with a mixed freight. WDs and 9Fs were commonplace right up to the end of steam working, but most were in a deplorable condition in the final years.

27.5.54

On a bright summer's evening B1 no. 61179 heads south with a fish train. The run down the 1-in-200 gradient from Abbots Ripton usually meant the locomotive would be shut off as the train neared Huntingdon station. No. 61179 was one of the batch of B1s built by Vulcan Foundry in 1947; it was withdrawn in January 1965.

8.9.59

In the mid-1950s a local pick-up goods ran south in the early evening from Huntingdon. Motive power was usually an L1 class 2–6–4T or a J6 0–6–0. No. 67797 was built by Robert Stephenson & Hawthorns and was completed in August 1950. It was just four years old when this picture was taken in Huntingdon goods yard while it was waiting to commence its journey south.

22.9.54

V2 no. 60948 heads a fast goods north. These locomotives with their 6ft 2in driving wheels were capable of a fair turn of speed, often being booked to work express trains. In the case of a locomotive failure it was likely that the replacement engine would be a V2, even on the heaviest trains.

28.3.63

When the Standard 9F 2–10–0s first arrived at New England they experienced some braking problems. A number of braking trials were undertaken, the first point being Huntingdon after descending the 1-in-200 gradient. This is no. 92038 shut off for the descent on a fine summer's evening; it has just passed the second of the Down line travelling post office lineside installations.

28.2.63

In their final complete decade of service a start was made on fitting A3s with double chimneys for the first time. A3 no. 60046 *Diamond Jubilee* received one in August 1958; the German-type smoke deflectors which gave the A3s a better appearance were later additions. They were fitted to no. 60046 in December 1961, just two years before withdrawal. The engine is seen heading an express at Huntingdon on a bright summer's evening.

6.7.59

A1 class no. 60138 *Boswell* was a York engine for many years until it was withdrawn in September 1965. It is seen here passing Huntingdon heading a semi-fast. Note the Esso tank wagons in the background: these were a familiar sight during the 1950s and 1960s. After withdrawal, no. 60138 spent two months in store before being cut up by Wards of Killamarsh.

24.2.63

Bright cold weather always improved the smoke effect from steam locomotives in action. Here, no. 60869, minus its front number plate, heads north with a fast goods at Huntingdon. This engine was to remain in service for just four more months, ending its days at Doncaster Works five months after withdrawal.

28.2.63

Locomotives making their final journey under their own steam were a familiar sight in the 1960s. This is no. 68991, taking on water at Huntingdon. This was the last of the J50 class to be built, being completed at Gorton Works in August 1939. It was withdrawn in August 1961, having had a comparatively short working life for a shunting locomotive.

8.61

This is A1 no. 60123 *H.A. Ivatt* leaving Huntingdon, heading an evening King's Cross–Peterborough semi-fast. It was a Leeds engine at the time. The A1 class, officially classified 8P, eventually totalled 50 locomotives, including the rebuilt *Great Northern* classified A1/1. Five members of the class were fitted with roller bearings. When this picture was taken, no one would have thought that this engine would end its working life eight years later just 4 miles from this spot.

5.7.54

Late on Friday 7 September 1962 A1 no. 60123 *H.A. Ivatt* ran into the back of a goods train just south of Offord station. The main line was closed for many hours while two heavy breakdown cranes lifted the locomotive and cleared the smashed wagons. On the following Sunday the A1 was moved to a siding north of Offord station ready for towing to Doncaster. Considerable damage had been done to the front of the engine. as a result of which the engine was condemned. It was the first member of the class to be withdrawn.

9.9.62

King's Cross depot was just a month away from closure when this picture of A4 no. 60021 *Wild Swan* was taken at Huntingdon. The engine was still in excellent external condition. Despite this it was not among those transferred to the Scottish Region. It was withdrawn in October 1963 and cut up at Doncaster Works just four months later.

8.5.63

A3 class locomotives from the Newcastle area still worked south on occasions during early 1963. No. 60083 *Sir Hugo* was a Heaton engine when it was photographed at Huntingdon. This A3 was in the final form, with double chimney and smoke deflectors. It ended its working life at Gateshead depot from where it was withdrawn in May 1964; it was cut up at a North Blyth scrapyard.

3.3.63

Only a handful of V2 class locomotives were fitted with double blastpipes and chimneys; the first was modified in March 1960 because the poor quality of the coal available at the time had led to steaming problems. No. 60862, seen here near Abbots Ripton, was modified in October 1961. Originally, it was planned to change the entire class, but the rapid introduction of diesel locomotives meant that only eight were completed. No. 60862 was withdrawn the month after this photograph was taken.

8.5.63

After the closure of King's Cross depot, I made every effort to record on film the remaining steam locomotives. A3 no. 60050 *Persimmon* was one of the few A3s still at New England, their principal duties at the time being the King's Cross local services. It is seen here approaching Huntingdon with an evening train. I had no way of knowing at the time that *Persimmon*'s withdrawal was just a short time away.

8. 5.63

In the early 1950s the King's Cross–Peterborough trains were worked by 'Pacifics'. Here, no. 60050 *Persimmon* heads the afternoon service. The locomotive was in a deplorable external condition. Note the first vehicle, an old bogie coach, long since out of passenger service. How it came to be in this train, or what it was used for, I never did find out.

28.3.63

Most A3s were in a poor state in early 1963, but no. 60044 *Melton* was in good external condition when it was photographed near Great Stukeley on a local passenger service. Even so, the writing was on the wall for this engine as just two months later it was withdrawn, ending its days on Doncaster Works scrap road in November 1963.

5.5.63

This was probably an exciting moment for the young engineman put in charge of watching the gauges on J15 no. 65475 as the breakdown gang from New England depot set about re-railing the engine. It had been de-railed near Huntingdon East while working a goods train to St Ives. Only the locomotive had come off the rails: the tender was unaffected.

3.8.55

J15 no. 65477 engaged in shunting at Huntingdon yard. This locomotive was built at Stratford Works and was completed in 1913, remaining in service until February 1960. This J15, like most of the Cambridge engines, was fitted with dual brakes, steam heat and screw couplings, although a considerable number of this class had steam brakes only.

17.9.54

Huntingdon East was a sub-shed of Cambridge, and it was used in the 1950s by the 'Huntingdon Pilot', a J15 class locomotive, changed on a ten-day rota basis. No. 65477 was a regular engine on this duty, but only on very rare occasions did it use the shed. Two sets of enginemen, all local, worked from here. The locomotive's duties included shunting and a local trip working to St Ives and back.

7.8.52

J15 no. 65442 runs through Huntingdon station pushing wagons collected from sidings north of the station. The open wooden wagons were typical of many thousands in service during the 1950s. The J15 class locomotives were powerful for their size and in their heyday, around the turn of the century, they were responsible for most of the goods traffic on the Great Eastern Railway before the arrival of larger engines.

12.9.54

This J15, no. 65420, is fitted with steam brakes only and three-link coupling. This was a Cambridge engine at this time and only on one or two occasions was it sent to Huntingdon. Built at Stratford and completed in January 1892, this engine had a long working life: it was not withdrawn until August 1962, a remarkable seventy years. It was among the last members of the class in service and it was used, ironically, to lift the Huntingdon–St Ives line.

14.6.56

This photograph is included because it shows several once-familiar railway structures at Huntingdon. Notice the signal, its arms low to enable them to be seen by drivers approaching the station from the north. In the background is the large water tank and chimney for the heating system; this has long since gone. J15 class no. 65461 was another of the regular engines on the pilot duty.

28.6.54

A4 no. 60030 *Golden Fleece* at Peterborough North station. At this time, the station still had an overall roof, with the platforms on a curve, so through non-stop trains ran under a speed restriction. The *Golden Fleece* was not stopping on this occasion, and has just reached the platform end. Note the burnished buffers: this was a King's Cross engine.

7.8.54

Track lifting in progress at Godmanchester: J15 no. 65420, a steam brake only example, stands ready to move off with another load of recovered track. The J15 ran to and from New England depot daily for servicing. This engine had just one more year in service, most of which was spent on this type of work.

31.8.61

The Huntingdon–St Ives line had severe weight restrictions owing to the many wooden trestle bridges similar to the one on which J15 no. 65420 is standing while engaged on track lifting. In the background is the large corn mill, once a well-known landmark but long since gone. Apart from the crossing-keeper's cottage, there is now no trace of the railway at Godmanchester, and the site is now lost under the very busy A14.

31.8.61

During the 1950s you could not travel far in East Anglia before coming across a 'Claud', as the D16 class was commonly known. No. 62529 is seen here travelling in fine style near St Ives with a parcels train. These engines were also responsible for local passenger workings over a wide area. No. 62529 was built at Stratford in 1902 as a D14 class; it was rebuilt as a D15 in 1929 and converted to D16/3 six years later. It was withdrawn from service in November 1959.

8.10.51

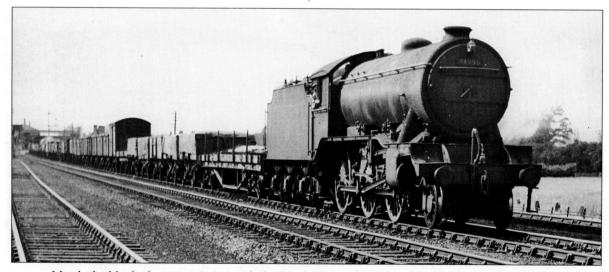

March shed had a long association with the K3 class 2–6–0s. Here, no. 61946 heads a mixed goods near St Ives en route to London. During the 1950s some of the K3s were moved away and replaced by the much later K1 class 2–6–0s introduced by A.H. Peppercorn in 1949, although some K3s remained here right through to the end of steam.

1.7.54

Nothing seemed to change the daily routine on cross country and branch lines, and keeping to time was seldom a problem as passenger levels changed little. Here, D16 no. 62569 waits for departure time at St Ives with the afternoon train to Cambridge. This is a typical example of the engines of this class which retained the original footplating on rebuilding.

1.7.54

A light load for K3 no. 61886 as it hurries along near St Ives with the afternoon parcels. This train enjoyed a variety of motive power, with 'Sandringhams', 'Clauds' and K3s the types mostly commonly seen. The large-boilered K3s had a tendency to rough riding, especially when they were due for a general overhaul.

1.7.54

No. 62036, one of the sizeable stud of K1 class 2–6–0s allocated to March depot, pulls out of the sidings at St Ives. The Peppercorn K1s were built by the North British Locomotive Company between 1949 and 1950, and this example remained in service until October 1963. Only one example of this class has made it into preservation.

24.6.54

The J17 class was designed for working loose-coupled goods trains, and as a result they had steam brakes only and three-link couplings. Much later, a few were equipped with vacuum ejectors and steam heating pipes. No. 65501, seen here with a small tender at St Ives, was originally built as a J16 and was completed at Stratford Works in September 1900. It was rebuilt as a J17 in April 1929. It was a King's Lynn engine when this picture was taken, and it remained in service until January 1958.

24.6.54

During the 1950s the white disc head codes were still widely used by locomotives on passenger services. This is D16/3 no. 62569, heading for Cambridge with the afternoon train. St Ives was a fairly busy junction, where the Kettering line via Huntingdon East joined, but no now trace of the railway exists here.

24.6.54

Five members of the J17 class were fitted with tender cabs during the 1950s; this was principally for working goods trains where reasonable runs of tender-first working were involved. This picture of no. 65575, which received its tender in 1952, shows clearly the modifications required to the locomotive cab roof to run with this type of tender. No. 65575 was completed in February 1906, remaining in service until February 1958.

17.3.54

The J19 class was introduced in 1916; ten locomotives were built prior to this as J18s and subsequently rebuilt to J19 specifications. No. 64650 was the first of the J19s, completed at Stratford in August 1916. As with all 25 examples it was later rebuilt with a round-topped boiler, in this case in 1937; this gave them a very similar appearance to the more numerous Gresley J39 class. The locomotive is working hard hauling a long train of coal empties bound for March on the long curve through St Ives station.

17.3.54

This peaceful scene at Mildenhall is typical of many rural branch lines that once existed in East Anglia. J15 no. 65451 simmers gently before its return working. The branch train consisted of two coaches and a parcel van. Services on the branch were worked by Cambridge depot engines, including E4s, J15s and Ivatt 2MT 2–6–0s.

31.5.56

On arrival at Mildenhall the first task was to release the engine from its train and turn it on the small turntable adjacent to the station. After coupling up again, the enginemen could relax until the time came for the return working to Cambridge. No. 65451 has a good head of steam, but the brickwork surrounding the turntable had seen better days.

31.5.56

Steam was escaping from the cylinders of V2 no. 60914 as it made a spirited start from Huntingdon. This locomotive was one of the batch allocated to King's Cross; it remained there until 1959 when it moved to New England. It was among the seventy V2s withdrawn in 1962. After a short period in store it was cut up at Doncaster Works.

13.6.57

L1 class 2–6–4T no. 67744 of Hitchin depot has been coaled up and is ready to set off from Huntingdon yards with an early evening pick-up goods. The L1 was one of the batch built by the North British Locomotive Company in 1948. The prototype engine was built at Doncaster in 1945 but production did not commence until 1948 at Darlington; later examples were built by the North British Locomotive Company and Robert Stephenson & Hawthorns, with the last 100 being completed in September 1950.

16.9.54

The V2 class engines were certainly 'maids of all work'. This is no. 60893 at Huntingdon, heading a heavy coal train bound for Ferme Park – a duty normally handled by a WD 2–8–0 or a Standard 9F 2–10–0. Engines of this class were equally at home heading an express, which they often did both on booked duties and as relief locomotives, taking over at short notice.

3.3.55

The streamlined W1 class 4–6–4 allocated to King's Cross was a regular sight on the East Coast main line during the early 1950s. It is pictured here at Huntingdon with an express. This historic locomotive was built in 1929 as a four-cylinder compound with a high pressure water tube boiler, and was rebuilt in 1937. In October 1953 this engine was transferred to Doncaster but still worked regularly into London, returning at 3.50 p.m. It survived a derailment at Peterborough in 1955, reappearing three months later, but it was withdrawn from service in June 1959.

7.8.52

A2/3 class no. 60500 *Edward Thompson*, pictured at Huntingdon with a King's Cross express. This was not a booked stop, hence the lack of activity on the station platform. The A2/3s were of new construction, being a development of the A2/2 introduced in 1946. The locomotive was fitted with the straight-sided double chimney which did little for its general appearance. No. 60500 was a New England engine for several years and was withdrawn when the depot closed in 1963.

6.9.53

On Sundays during the early 1950s a fast goods passed Huntingdon at around 9 a.m., usually worked by a K3 class locomotive. No. 61890 is seen here at speed with a clear road ahead. The sparse traffic at that time usually resulted in a fast run to London unless engineering work was in progress.

8.7.53

Several classes of ex-Great Northern Railway 0–6–0s were still active in the early 1950s, albeit in rapidly declining numbers (with the exception of the J6 class). The J1 class was introduced by H.A. Ivatt in 1908; only fifteen were built, all in that year, at Doncaster Works. Withdrawals commenced in 1947. By early 1954 only two remained. One of these was no. 65013 seen here at Huntingdon, having arrived with an engineer's train. This engine was allocated to Hitchin and used principally on this work. When this picture was taken its days were numbered, and no. 65013, the last survivor of the class, was withdrawn in November 1954.

9.9.54

With the tell-tale signs of overfilling on its tankside, L1 class no. 67744 prepares to back on to a pick-up goods which was its next duty. At Hitchin depot L1s and J6 0–6–0s were the normal motive power although for a short period ex-LMS Fowler 2–6–4Ts appeared on loan. The L1s, with their 5ft 2in driving wheels, were usually employed on local passenger work, and they were capable of a fair turn of speed.

16.9.54

Huntingdon East station was on a sharp curve, hence the check rails. Only on very rare occasions would the J6 booked for the southbound pick-up goods go in to take water, but no. 64186 had done so. It then had to wait for a suitable gap in traffic in order to cross over the main lines to get to the goods yard.

12.5.55

The cleaners at Hitchin depot seem to have had a go at J6 no. 64206 although no one had cleaned the number on the cab side. These robust 0–6–0s first appeared in 1911, and over an eleven-year period 110 examples were built. Despite being classified 3F they were often used on passenger trains. No. 64206 was completed at Doncaster in June 1913 and withdrawn in September 1960.

5.8.55

On several Sundays during the summer an excursion ran from King's Cross to Skegness, hauled by a B1 class 4–6–0. No. 61266 is seen here leaving Huntingdon. In those days excursions such as this were very popular as few people had their own cars. The B1 was fitted with electric lighting although lamps were also in use.

14.8.52

In the early 1950s there was only one stopping train from Peterborough to London on a Sunday morning, departing Huntingdon just after 9 a.m. New England B1 no. 61389 was in charge of this service and is seen here making a spirited start. In those days there were more stations on the main line, and its next stop was at Offord, long since closed and demolished.

26.10.52

One of Sir Nigel Gresley's finest designs was his mixed traffic 2–6–2, officially classified V2. These were powerful engines and their 6ft 2in driving wheels made them capable of working express trains. They were equally at home on the heaviest goods. Here, no. 60849 heads for London with a typical mixed goods of that period.

5.7.54

Three of the A2/2 class 4–6–2s rebuilt from Gresley's P2 class 2–8–2s were allocated to New England; the other three were based at York. On occasions these engines worked the Sunday morning Peterborough–King's Cross working. Here, no. 60506 *Wolf of Badenoch* leaves Huntingdon amid clouds of steam. The A2/2s were not particularly successful locomotives, most of their duties being semi-fasts and locals. These engines ran with rimmed chimneys and smoke lifters in the early 1950s, and all but one later received a more attractive lipped chimney.

8.3.53

There were few passengers on the early local services on Sundays. The first northbound train from King's Cross arrived around 10 a.m., usually worked by a Pacific which would return with an express. A4 no. 60032 *Gannet* is seen approaching Huntingdon with a three-coach train. The A4 was fitted with a single chimney at this time, receiving a double one in November 1958. No. 60032 was withdrawn from New England depot in October 1963.

11.7.54

Locomotives from Colwick depot, Nottingham, were not common on the main line south of Peterborough but they were occasionally to be seen on Sunday mornings heading a fast goods to London. K3 no. 61824 had just taken water and was awaiting the signal at Huntingdon. The K3s with their large boilers had a tendency to rough riding as they became due for general overhaul.

11.7.54

No. 60022 *Mallard*, the world speed record holder for steam power, was a King's Cross engine for many years, right up until withdrawal in April 1963. Here it is seen heading the Sunday morning King's Cross–Peterborough train of just four coaches. The return working would have been very different, taking over a heavy express for the final leg of the journey.

4.7.54

Most locomotives shut off steam for the down gradient from Abbots Ripton, but not V2 no. 60876 which was going in fine style heading a fast goods. Note the burnt patch at the base of the smokebox door, and the leading wagon used to transport livestock. These were still commonplace in the 1950s, and most stations, even small ones, had a cattle-loading dock.

4.3.55

A1 class no. 60136 *Alcazar* was one of a batch of eleven members of the class allocated to Grantham depot in the mid-1950s. The A1s were powerful locomotives designed by A.H. Peppercorn, and were a development of the A1/1 *Great Northern* rebuilt by E. Thompson in 1945. The production run of these engines did not begin until 1948, with a total of forty-nine being built. A1s were excellent engines, but were somewhat overshadowed by the Pacifics designed by Sir Nigel Gresley.

7.8.52

V2s were capable of handling the heaviest expresses: here, V2 no. 60975 has just taken over the King's Cross–Edinburgh at Peterborough and is getting the train under way. The station was on a curve, and northbound expresses required the services of a banker. In the early 1950s this work was performed by elderly C12 class 4–4–2Ts which made a deafening noise as they blasted their way through the station with its overall roof.

5.9.53

An immaculate C12 4–4–2T no. 67365 in fully lined livery drifts into Peterborough at the head of a train of outer suburban stock which a B1 or V2 would take over for the journey to King's Cross. The C12s were designed by H.A. Ivatt and introduced in 1898 principally for working suburban trains. During the early 1950s a number were to be found at New England, their duties including working as station pilots and local branch line passenger services.

5.9.53

Peterborough North with a typical Midland & Great Northern train of the period. B12 no. 61537 was a South Lynn engine when this picture was taken, but later several B12s moved to Yarmouth Beach shed. Note the tablet exchange apparatus mounted on the front of the tender. Note also the empty pigeon crates, once a familiar sight at stations, on their way back to the pigeon fanciers.

5.9.53

K2 class locomotives from Boston depot were frequently used on passenger services during the early 1950s. Twelve members of the class were allocated to the shed, including no. 61731, seen here arriving at Peterborough North. Built at Doncaster Works in 19194, it remained in service until June 1959.

7.8.54

Peterborough's Spital Bridge depot was originally part of the London Midland Region, transferring to the Eastern in 1950. Many of the ex-London Midland locomotives remained there right up to closure. In the intervening period Eastern Region B1 4–6–0s, D16 4–4–0s and C12 4–4–2Ts were among the engines allocated there. 4F no. 44182 is seen here in the depot yard.

13.5.55

Great activity at Peterborough around A3 no. 60106 *Flying Fox*, in charge of the 'London & North Eastern Flier', which it had worked from King's Cross. The A3 was a New England engine, King's Cross depot having closed the previous year. It was fitted with a double chimney and German-type deflectors. *Flying Fox* was withdrawn in December 1964 and was cut up at King's scrapyard, Norwich.

2.5.64

New England's overhead water system gantry can be clearly seen in this picture. No. 61138 stands in company with one of the depot's Standard 9F 2–10–0s. New England was one of the largest Eastern Region depots in the mid-1950s, with around 170 locomotives on its books, most of them heavy freight types.

6.7.59

With steam shut off for the approach to Peterborough, A1 no. 60136 *Alcazar* passes the travelling post office installations at Walton. The A1 was in charge of a Leeds–King's Cross train. *Alcazar* was withdrawn in May 1963, ending its days on the scraproad at Doncaster Works that same month.

6.9.64

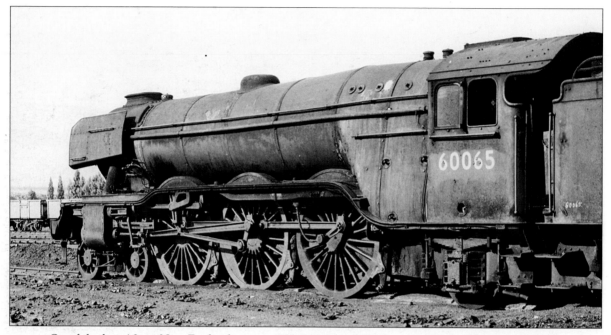

On of the last A3s at New England was no. 60065 *Knight of Thistle*, seen here in the shed yard in a very run-down condition. The nameplates have already been removed. This locomotive had been condemned the previous month but it was to remain at New England for two months after withdrawal before being towed to King's scrapyard, Norwich.

30.8.64

Another picture of no. 60065 *Knight of Thistle* at New England. Rather surprisingly, although the engine was already withdrawn, the tender was still full of coal, and the front number plate remained (but not the nameplates). Several A3s ended their working days at New England, where their final duties included semi-fast services to King's Cross.

6.7.59

Change-over day, and C12 no. 67350 returns at a leisurely pace to New England after a stint on branch line duty. The C12s with their 5ft 8in driving wheels were capable of a fair turn of speed. Sixty members of this class were built, all at Doncaster; no. 67350 was the prototype, completed in February 1898. Forty-nine C12s were taken into British Railways stock. No. 67350 was withdrawn in April 1955.

14.8.54

The six A2/2 engines started life as P2 class 2–8–2s to the design of Sir Nigel Gresley; rebuilding by Edward Thompson commenced in 1943. By the early 1950s they were equally divided between York and New England. No. 60504 *Mons Meg* was one of those allocated to the latter depot. The three Eastern Region engines were mostly used on King's Cross local trains and fast goods. No. 60504 was withdrawn in January 1961. All six A2/2s were cut up at Doncaster.

13.3.55

Examples of the J6 0–6–0 were commonplace at New England in the 1950s; this is hardly surprising as twenty-eight members of the class were allocated there, well over a quarter of the total. They were used on a wide variety of work, including shunting and trip workings to and from the brickworks which were numerous in those days. Others worked pick-up goods and engineers' trains. No. 64211 is pictured on shed in company with a J52 0–6–0ST.

13.3.55

Another of New England's J6s, no. 64254. This engine was fitted with tablet exchange apparatus at the front of the tender for working on parts of the Midland & Great Northern. Some wag had chalked the phrase 'Miserere Me!' on the smokebox door. No. 64254 was withdrawn in October 1959. The depot's overhead water supply gantry can be seen in the background.

13.3.55

By the end of the 1950s the locomotive stock at New England had gone down considerably, with twenty-five Standard 9F 2–10–0s accounting for almost a quarter of the depot's allocation. The Ivatt 4MT 2–6–0 behind no. 92149 was one of six to be found at the shed.

6.7.59

A4 no. 60017 *Silver Fox*, a King's Cross engine, gathers speed as it passes Walton; ahead lies the Stoke Bank climb. No. 60017 was completed at Doncaster Works in December 1935. When this picture was taken it still had the single chimney; it received the double version in May 1957. Withdrawal from service came in October 1963, and it ended its days at its birthplace the following year.

14.8.54

With the long run down Stoke Bank behind it, no. 60022 *Mallard* could take it easy on the approach to Peterborough, heading a heavy Newcastle–King's Cross express. The headboard from its outward journey can be seen reversed above the locomotive's smokebox number plate. No. 60022 was one of the handful of A4s built with a double chimney.

14.8.54

A4 no. 60008 *Dwight D. Eisenhower* seen here at Walton going well with 'The Flying Scotsman'. This locomotive was originally named *Golden Shuttle*, being renamed in September 1945. As with all the A4s fitted with single chimneys, it was later to receive a double version. This A4 has survived into preservation in the United States.

14.8.54

Many of the powerful Standard 9F 2–10–0s had short working lives owing to the headlong rush to change over to diesel traction. Here, no. 92171 heads past Walton with a heavy goods. This engine was one of the large batch allocated to New England depot which was only four months away from closure when this picture was taken. Its closure marked the end of the line for many of the 9Fs.

6.9.94

Some B1s ended their working life in very poor external condition; this was certainly the case with no. 61109 seen here at New England. Note the old Great Northern tender and the shunter's pole on the locomotive's buffer beam. No. 61109 was one of the batch built by the North British Locomotive Company in 1946, ending its working days in July 1964.

6.7.59

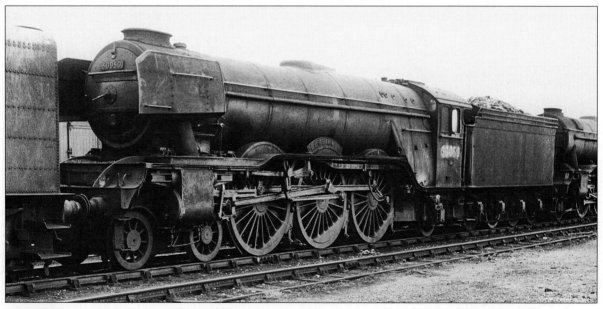

In June 1963 King's Cross depot closed to steam. Shortly afterwards a number of Pacifics and V2s could be seen withdrawn in a siding at New England. No. 60050 *Persimmon* awaits it final journey, its tender still at that time full of coal. The number on the cab side could still be seen through all the dirt and grime mainly through a cleaner's efforts.

23.6.63

The withdrawn A3s in line at New England included no. 60044 *Melton*. These engines were towed to Doncaster for cutting up. Rather surprisingly, all had lost their shedplates, though their front number and nameplates were still intact. Presumably at some stage there was the possibility of transfer elsewhere.

23.6.63

During the early 1950s most V2s were in good external condition, but this was definitely not the case with no. 60893, seen here with a local passenger train approaching Walton crossing. No. 60893 was built at Darlington Works during the Second World War, and was completed in January 1940 at a time when extra motive power was urgently needed. It completed twenty-three years' service before withdrawal.

14.8.54

Among the V2s at New England in June 1963 awaiting their final journey was no. 60854. This design was unquestionably one of Sir Nigel Gresley's finest. Despite very little maintenance, these engines were often called upon to work very heavy trains during the war, in the process acquiring the nickname 'war winners'.

23.6.63

The early 1960s were a sad time for steam enthusiasts. Many fine engines were laid aside and replaced by diesels, a number of which were themselves quickly to disappear. No. 60803, seen here at New England, was one of the first batch of V2s built. It was completed in October 1936 just four months after the well-known *Green Arrow*. The last example of the 184-strong class was completed at Darlington in July 1944.

23.6.63

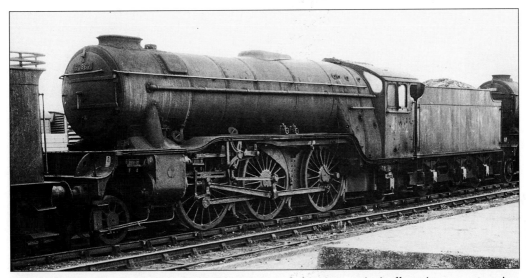

Only eight V2s were fitted with double blastpipes and chimneys, principally to improve steaming which was being adversely affected by the poor quality of coal available in the early 1960s. No. 60862 was modified in October 1961. The change improved the V2s' performance and it was intended to modify all members of the class. However, only eight were modified, principally because of the rapid change-over to diesel power.

23.6.63

During the early 1950s New England had more C12 class 4–4–2Ts than it had duties for them. As a result one or more could always be seen in store. Here, no. 67366, accompanied by a J52 0–6–0ST, stands in the shed yard. The C12 was eventually returned to traffic and withdrawn in April 1958. The locomotive's chimney had been covered with a piece of old tarpaulin, in the manner usual at the time.

13.3.55

The piece of tarpaulin lying near the smokebox suggests that no. 67352 is about to be put into, or has just been retrieved from, storage. It was certainly not about to be withdrawn as this engine remained in service until November 1958.

13.3.55

Surplus or withdrawn locomotives were often used as stationary boilers at depots, as with J52 no. 68817 seen here supplying steam at New England. This locomotive was built by Robert Stephenson & Company in 1899; it was still in service when this picture was taken and was not officially withdrawn until April 1958. J52s were once commonplace on the Eastern Region and could be seen in considerable numbers at Peterborough and in the outer suburbs of London.

13.3.55

The appearance of A2/3 no. 60500 *Edward Thompson* was considerably improved by the fitting of a lipped double chimney. This was another of the withdrawn engines to be seen at New England in June 1963. No. 60500 (or 500 as it was in LNER days) was completed at Doncaster Works in May 1946. Just a few days later at Marylebone it was named *Edward Thompson*, after the locomotive's designer and the Chief Mechanical Engineer of the LNER 1941–6. The engine fell victim to a cutting torch at Doncaster in September 1963.

23.6.63

Interest in the few remaining steam engines on the southern section of the Eastern Region was at a low ebb in 1962/3, with the notable exception of the King's Cross A4s, until that depot closed. The generally run-down state of A2/3 no. 60520 *Owen Tudor* at New England indicates that the engine had certainly not been cleaned for some time. Such was the hurry to take it out of service its tender was still filled to capacity.

23.6.63

Four A2/3s were laid aside at New England. No. 60523 *Sun Castle* was built at Doncaster, being completed in August 1947. This engine spent several years allocated to New England during the 1950s, with a two-year spell at Doncaster. In their heyday the A2/3s were to be seen on principal expresses but with the arrival of the Peppercorn A1s they mostly worked secondary duties.

23.6.63

This locomotive is a good example of the A.H. Peppercorn A2s. No. 60533 *Happy Knight* was completed in April 1948; it emerged from Doncaster Works numbered 60533 and received a double chimney in December 1949, two months after the well-known survivor *Blue Peter* received its modification. *Happy Knight* was based at New England on several occasions during the 1950s with spells at Grantham and Doncaster. In its final years the A2 spent much of its time on local passenger duties.

23.6.63

The five examples of the Y4 class 0–4–0Ts were built at Stratford Works for the Great Eastern Railway to the design of A.J. Hill. Their sturdy workman-like appearance made them look like a more recent design. All five were to be found at Stratford in the 1950s. No. 68125, seen here at Stratford, was completed in November 1913. It was the first to be withdrawn, being condemned in September 1955. The last survivor remained in service stock until December 1963.

7.5.55

'Sandringham' class no. 61662 *Manchester United* was a Colchester engine when it was photographed at Stratford. Officially classified B17/4, it was fitted with a straight-sided 4,200 gallon tender. Built by Robert Stephenson & Company, it was completed in January 1937 and withdrawn in December 1959. Sadly no examples of the B17s or the rebuilt B2s have survived into preservation.

7.5.55

Two D16s await the scrapman's torch at Stratford. No. 62573, from King's Lynn, had been condemned the previous month. There is still coal in the tender and the white headcode disc is still in place. Sadly, no examples of this class survived into preservation. They were a feature of East Anglia, and elsewhere, for many years.

13.11.55

The D16/3s were widely known as 'Clauds'. No. 62585 was a Cambridge engine regularly working services to Bletchley where it was often to be seen on shed during the day. It is pictured here at Stratford Works immediately after being condemned. The chimney, dome cover, coupling rods and part of the cab roof have already gone.

7.5.55

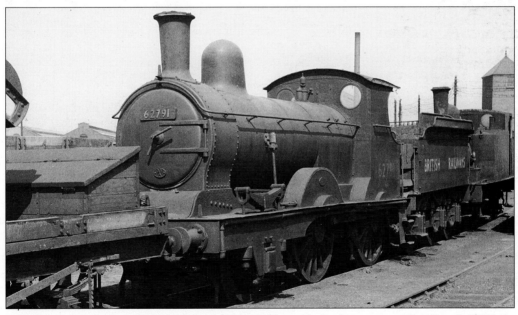

Withdrawn E4 class no. 62791 of Cambridge shed stands in the scrap road at Stratford Works awaiting its fate, its tender still lettered British Railways. The E4s were the only 2–4–0 tender design in service at this time. They had 5ft 8in driving wheels and were capable of a fair turn of speed, and were originally introduced by the Great Eastern Railway for express work.

7.5.55

While Stratford was busy cutting up D16s in 1955 examples were still going through works for general overhaul. This is no. 62544 shining like a new pin in its glossy black lined-out livery. Also fresh from works overhaul was J19 class no. 64655. Shunting was being carried out by a B1 class 4–6–0 under the watchful eye of the shunter in charge.

7.5.55

Lincoln J39 class 0–6–0 no. 64722 stands in the yard at Stratford Works fresh from a general overhaul. The J39s were designed by Sir Nigel Gresley and introduced to the LNER in 1926. In all 289 were built at Darlington Works, with a further 28 by Beyer Peacock in 1936/7. The J39s were used on goods and passenger work.

7.5.55

Twelve of these J70 class 0–6–0T tram engines were built at Stratford Works for the Great Eastern Railway between 1903 and 1921; all but one survived to be taken into British Railways stock. They will be long associated with the Wisbech & Upwell Tramway. This one, no. 68222, remained there as a reserve engine after diesels had taken over. Other members of the class were to be found at Yarmouth, Colchester and Ipswich. No. 68222 was withdrawn in January 1955, and the class as a whole became extinct just seven months later.

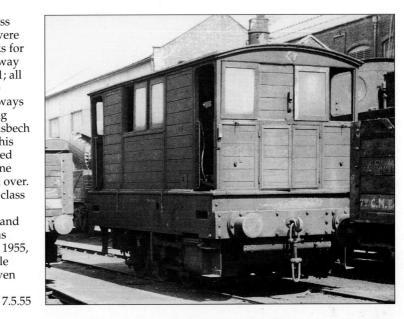

7.5.55

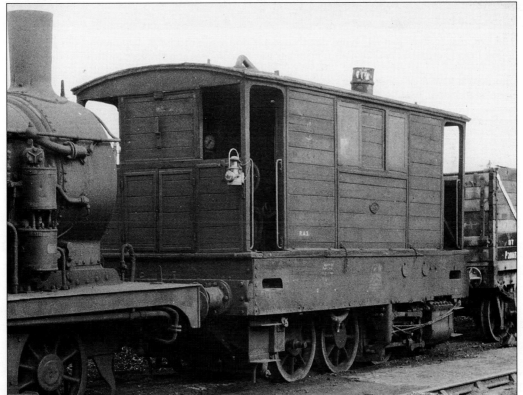

Also awaiting its fate at Stratford Works in 1955 was J70 no. 68225, seen here in company with a withdrawn F4 2–4–2T. This engine was condemned in March of that year. The coupling rods have been removed and part of the valve gear tied up to enable it to be towed on its final journey to Stratford Works where it was built in 1921.

7.5.55

The ex-Great Eastern 0–6–0Ts were distributed far and wide in LNER days, with examples to be found in the north-east and Scotland. J68 no. 68661 is seen here at a smoky Stratford shed. The J68s were designed by A.J. Hill and introduced in 1912; in total thirty were built, and all but one made it into British Railways service. The class was designed for working suburban trains from Liverpool Street station. No. 68661 later moved to Hitchin and was withdrawn from there in December 1959.

7.5.55

Stratford was the largest shed in the Eastern Region with over 400 engines in the mid-1950s. Many were ex-Great Eastern designs, among them a number of J15 class 0–6–0s. No. 65449, built in September 1899, was an example of the class fitted with Westinghouse brakes and vacuum ejector. At 1 January 1948 127 J15s passed into British Railways ownership. This example remained in service until December 1959.

7. 5.55

The locomotive engineers of the Great Eastern Railway were great believers in 2–4–2 tank designs. The F5 class was introduced in 1904 principally for suburban services. Thirty-two F5s were taken into British Railways stock; these included two re-designated from class F6. During the war several of these engines, together with F4s, had been used by the government in various parts of the country, some even being armour-plated to work with coastal defence units. By the mid-1950s there was little work for the remaining 2–4–2Ts. No. 67192 was photographed at Stratford lying idle; it was withdrawn in April 1958.

7.5.55

3P 4–4–2T no. 41970 was officially allocated to Southend Victoria shed in 1955 but was stored at Stratford. These engines were widely used on the London Tilbury Southend line. By the mid-1950s they had mostly been succeeded by later designs but odd examples were still receiving general overhauls at Devons Road works.

7.5.55

This J17 class 0–6–0 no. 65508 started life in 1900 as a J16, being rebuilt as a J17 in LNER days. It is seen here at Stratford Works fitted with a tender weatherboard. It had steam brakes only with the usual three-link coupling. Stratford had fourteen examples of the class in the mid-1950s, including no. 65508. It was withdrawn from service in June 1958. Fortunately one example of the J17s made it into preservation.

7.5.55

The 'flowerpot'-type chimney was fitted to the majority of the N7s. No. 69732 was built at Gorton Works in 1926. It was fitted with Westinghouse pump and vacuum ejector, being rebuilt with a round-topped firebox in 1943. The Stratford N7s were mostly used on suburban services from Liverpool Street. Stratford had no fewer than ninety-three in the mid-1950s. No. 69732 remained in service until September 1962, ten years after the first of the class had made its final journey.

7.5.55

Wherever you looked at Stratford in the early 1950s there were engines: this was hardly surprising with over 400 locomotives on its books, ranging from 'Britannias' to the tiny Y4 0–4–0Ts. N7 no. 69601, built in 1915, was originally fitted with condensers but these were removed in 1936. The engine was evidently undergoing repairs when this picture was taken; parts are to be seen lying on the running plate, and the smokebox is tied with string. It was fitted with the more attractive straight-sided chimney. Note also the clean rim on the smokebox door.

7.5.55

Fresh from general overhaul at Stratford Works this is no. 69722; it had no distance to travel back to its home shed as it was one of the large number allocated to Stratford. This engine was one of the batch built at Doncaster, and was completed in June 1928. The condensing gear was removed in 1937. No. 69722 managed just five more years in service; it was withdrawn in the sizeable batch condemned in December 1960.

7.5.55

On the part of the Cambridge shed area commonly known as 'The Dump' by enthusiasts, you could find engines travelling to and from works, en route to new depots, awaiting repair or simply waiting for their next duty. C12 class no. 67397 was a Bury St Edmunds engine at the time so was presumably at Cambridge for repairs. It remained in service until December 1958, achieving fifty-one years' service.

2.8.55

A stranger in the camp! While E4 class 2–4–0s were commonplace at Cambridge, those allocated to Norwich were unusual. This is no. 62792 in a generally run-down state, although the smokebox and chimney had received a coat of paint. (This was usually done after light repairs and was more often seen on the London Midland Region.) Of the 100 members of the class built between 1891 and 1902, only eighteen made it into British Railways stock. No. 62792 was withdrawn in June 1956.

2.8.55

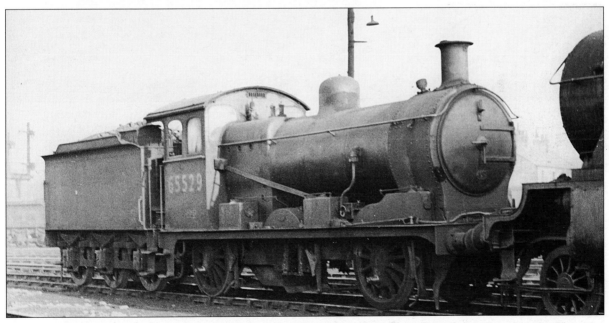

J17 class no. 65529 in trouble, having run hot. The middle set of driving wheels had been removed, with various parts left on the running board as the locomotive was towed out and dumped in the yard until ready for re-assembly. Its chimney appears to have seen better days, the rim having almost disappeared. Note also there is no number plate at this time. Despite these problems no. 65529 remained in service until May 1958.

14.11.51

Bury St Edmunds 'Claud' no. 62615 having just arrived at Cambridge. The guard, his duty done, is making his way down the platform, lamp in hand. Once released from the train, the engine would go on shed for servicing. Note the tell-tale signs on the bottom of the smokebox door (albeit painted over) that the engine has been worked hard. Nevertheless this engine had four more years in service before being withdrawn.

13.7.54

The 'Clauds' allocated to Bury St Edmunds were regular visitors to Cambridge. No. 62576 is typical of those rebuilt with a larger round-topped boiler and modified footplating; these modifications were completed on this locomotive in March 1937. Massive inroads were made into the D16/3s in the late 1950s. This example was withdrawn in September 1957 and cut up at Stratford.

9.5.55

There were several versions of the 'Clauds' to be seen in the late 1950s, all classified D16/3; the few remaining D15s and D16/2s had been withdrawn earlier. No. 62540 was a rebuild of a D15 with a larger round-topped boiler and modified footplating; rebuilding to D16/3 specification was done in June 1934. When this picture was taken at Cambridge it was a Norwich engine and had just four weeks more in service.

2.8.55

'Sandringham' class no. 61635 *Milton* coaled up and ready to depart from Cambridge with a March local train. The first withdrawal of a B17 was no. 61628 *Harewood House* in September 1952. Only odd examples were withdrawn prior to 1958 when large inroads were made into the class, no. 61635 going in January 1959. The building on the right is the locomotive shed.

31.5.56

On occasions in the early 1950s Stratford depot K3s were used on the Liverpool Street–Cambridge trains. No. 61963 has just arrived, uncoupled, and is ready to move off to the shed for water and coal supplies. Note the express code: white discs were in regular use in East Anglia at the time. While the K3s were powerful engines they had a reputation for rough riding, especially when running fast; one wonders how the enginemen had fared with this example on the run from London.

18.9.54

During the mid-1950s Cambridge had a stud of ten B1 4–6–0s. Their regular duties included London trains to both Liverpool Street and King's Cross, which had previously been mostly worked by 'Sandringhams'. Here, no. 61285 stands ready to leave Cambridge with a stopping train to Norwich.

18.9.54

A wide range of motive power was to be seen on Cambridge station pilot duties. At the time this picture was taken E4s and ex-Great Eastern 0–6–0Ts were the most usual. 'Claud' no. 62518 of King's Lynn depot had been commandeered. Note the mixed stock, especially the coach on the line behind the engine.

18.9.54

March 'Claud' no. 62542 runs into the bay platform at Cambridge. In the background is an immaculate B1, no. 61223, one of those allocated to 31A at the time this picture was taken. There was a rich variety of locomotives to be seen at Cambridge in the early 1950s, ranging from elderly Great Eastern types to B1s and 'Britannias'.

18.9.54

B1 class no. 61287 stands ready to leave for King's Cross. The coaching stock on the left was for a Bletchley train. While B1s generally took over many of the 'Sandringham' duties, including the King's Cross service, the latter engines were still to be seen on these duties on occasions. B1 no. 61287 was built by the North British Locomotive Company in 1948, remaining in service until September 1962.

13.7.54

Double-heading was not common on the Eastern Region where it was usually the result of engine failure. B1 class no. 61105 and V2 class no. 60800 *Green Arrow* await departure time from Cambridge with a King's Cross train. Both were in steam, so presumably this opportunity was being taken of working the V2 back to its home shed.

10.4.53

B2 class no. 61617 *Ford Castle* was one of ten B17 'Sandringhams' rebuilt by Edward Thompson between 1945 and 1947. This one was rebuilt in December 1946. *Ford Castle* was a reserve 'royal' engine allocated to Cambridge with B2 no. 61671 *Royal Sovereign*, the official engine. All ten B2s were withdrawn in 1958/9, no. 61617 being condemned in August 1958. The tender fitted to this engine is interesting as it is from an ex-North Eastern C7 class 'Atlantic'.

23.6.57

D16/3 no. 62576 photographed shortly after arrival at Cambridge with a March train. The long building in the background is part of the locomotive depot; it was possible to walk up to the far end of the platform from where the interior of the shed could be easily seen. Sadly no examples of the D16/3 made it into preservation, although these engines were once to be seen all over East Anglia and further afield.

9.5.55

E4 class 2–4–0 no. 62783 has just arrived at Cambridge with a train from Mildenhall. During the 1950s most of the remaining E4s were allocated to the depot. Their duties included branch line passenger trains, local pick-up goods and station pilot work. In the early 1950s there was a surplus of these engines and two were usually to be seen in store.

13.7.54

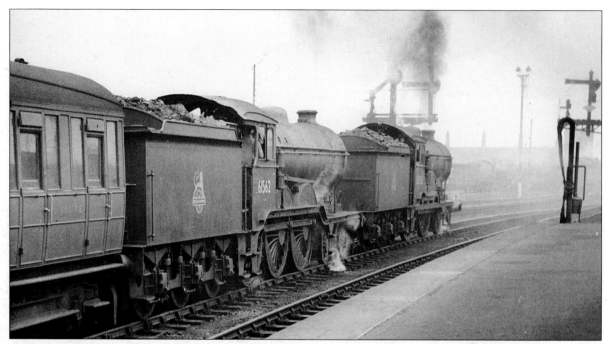

Double-heading was seldom seen on the Eastern Region as locomotives were generally capable of handling trains unaided. There were, of course, some occasions when, owing to locomotive failure, another engine was called up to haul the entire train to its destination. In this instance the most likely explanation was to work a crippled engine back to its home shed. D16 no. 62552 and B12 no. 61562 were both Ipswich engines.

9.5.55

On a grey dismal day D16 no. 62566 leaves Cambridge with a Bury St Edmunds train. The weather conditions were responsible for the clouds of smoke hanging over the depot. D16s with their 7ft driving wheels were capable of a fair turn of speed. At one time they were used on principal trains but by the 1950s were mostly relegated to secondary duties.

9.5.55

On arrival at Chesterton Junction civil engineer's depot to photograph the Sentinel locomotive no. 42 used for shunting, I was surprised to find it undergoing repairs in the open. Part of the engine can be seen on the right, pieces lie all around, and clothes are hanging from all available places! No. 42 was eventually returned to working order.

10.10.55

D16 no. 62613, pictured under the sheer legs at Yarmouth South Town depot ready to be lifted; the massive chains are already in place. The particular D16 was to move to Peterborough Spital Bridge and then on to March, from where it was withdrawn in November 1960. By that time, it was the sole survivor of its class.

18.8.57

E4 no. 62784 leaves the bay platform with the 11.05 a.m. for Colchester, consisting of just one coach. The locomotive was coupled to a tender commonly known as a 'watercart'. These were originally built for 'Claud Hamilton' class engines, and this was the last engine to run with this type of tender. Time was running out for this E4 as it was withdrawn the same month as this picture was taken.

9.5.55

The 'Royal' engine, B2 class no. 61671 *Royal Sovereign*, was kept in immaculate condition as it could be called upon at short notice. When this happened it was taken off its normal duties, given an extra special clean and the cab roof painted white. When it was on royal duties, a fitter, dressed in a suit, rode on the footplate, his overalls in a case. No. 61671 was originally named *Manchester City* but was renamed in 1946; it remained in service until September 1958.

17.5.52

During the early 1950s L1 class 2–6–4Ts worked into Cambridge from several depots, principally King's Cross, Hitchin and Stratford. No. 67730 was one of the twenty allocated to the latter shed. The last of the batch built at Darlington, it was completed in August 1948. After this, production switched to two private companies, the North British Locomotive Company and Robert Stephenson & Hawthorns.
13.7.54

Old traditions die hard! Despite the electric lighting fitted to B1 no. 61287, headlamps are still being used. This B1 has just finished taking on water at Cambridge prior to working the Cambridge buffet express to King's Cross. Trains for this destination regularly used the south end bay platform.
13.7.54

One of the Cambridge depot's B1 class 4–6–0s no. 61121 runs through the station to pick up its train for King's Cross. Note the coaches in the background which included many veteran examples in the early 1950s; they were a familiar sight around Cambridge.

13.7.54

The afternoon March–Cambridge train usually consisted of just three coaches in the 1950s. On this occasion 'Claud' no. 62531, a Cambridge engine, is shown leaving St Ives with an extra coach and van. This engine was among the first of the D16/3s to be withdrawn; it was condemned in March 1955 and cut up at Stratford Works.

1.7.54

The mid-afternoon Cambridge–March passenger train was a return working for a March engine. D16/3 no. 62539 is seen here in good external condition heading the service. 'Clauds' were to be found throughout East Anglia on such duties. Locomotives from Cambridge worked through to Bletchley while those at Peterborough Spital Bridge worked up into the Midlands.

1.7.54

Originally built for suburban workings, the C12 class 4–4–2Ts finished their working days on branch lines and empty stock duties. No. 67360 is seen here at Cambridge; it was one of three allocated there at the time, although one was usually in store. The C12s moved away not long after this picture was taken. No. 67360 remained in service until January 1955.

10.4.53

The Great Eastern Railway relied upon the 0–6–0 wheel arrangement for its freight workings. The J19 class was a development of the J17; they were later rebuilt with round-topped fireboxes. In all thirty-five were built, all of which made it into British Railways stock. The class remained intact until December 1958, but all were withdrawn by the end of 1962. No. 64673, pictured here at Bury St Edmunds, was among the last; it was condemned in August 1962.

2.7.55

Turning a locomotive by hand was not an easy job. D16/3 no. 62543 only just fits on the turntable at Bury St Edmunds depot. This shed came within the Cambridge district and had an allocation of only sixteen engines, seven of which were D16s. The shed closed in January 1959 and its locomotives were transferred to Cambridge.

2.7.55

F6 2–4–2T no. 67237 out to grass at Bury St Edmunds. When this picture was taken it had not worked for some time, and it was condemned in August the same year. The F6s had a long association with Cambridge and Bury St Edmunds in later years. The last example of the Great Eastern 2–4–2Ts disappeared in 1958.

2.5.55

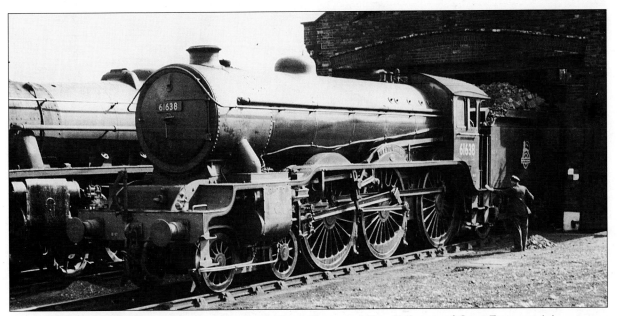

The three locomotive depots at Yarmouth, South Town and Vauxhall were of Great Eastern origin, while Yarmouth Beach was a Midland & Great Northern Railway shed. In British Railways days all four came within the Norwich district. 'Sandringham' no. 61638 *Melton Hall* was photographed at Vauxhall, alongside a summer visitor, a 'Black Five' from the London Midland Region with an excursion train.

18.8.57

D16/3 no. 62540 of Norwich shed awaits its next duty at Yarmouth South Town. This was the last of the three Yarmouth sheds to remain in use; it closed in November 1959. D16/3 no. 62540 was condemned in August that same year from Norwich where it had been based for a number of years.

18.8.57

Smoke control must have been very important at Yarmouth Beach depot owing to the proximity of the private houses nearby. In its final years the shed building was without a roof. The depot's allocation was eleven engines, although visitors working in with excursions would be serviced. No. 62524 was allocated to Yarmouth South Town when this picture was taken.

18.8.57

The dilapidated building at Yarmouth Beach can be seen in the background. J17 no. 65586 was among the last of the class to be built, being completed at Stratford in December 1910. It gave fifty-two years' service. Note the tender exchange apparatus fitted on the front of the tender. The sign outside the shed presumably warned of the limited clearance. In the background can be seen an Ivatt 4MT 2–6–0; these engines were familiar on M&GN services.

18.8.57

J39 class no. 64802, pictured here at Yarmouth Beach, was a Melton Constable engine. This was a larger shed with an allocation of twenty-five engines in the mid-1950s, well over half of which were Ivatt 2–6–0s, the mainstay of motive power on the Midland & Great Northern line. The J39s were a later introduction and were used on goods and passenger services. No. 64802 was condemned in July 1960.

18.8.57

In the 1950s these two B12s, nos 61520 and 61530, were allocated to Yarmouth Beach. Of the two, no. 61530 remained in service the longer; it was withdrawn in November 1959, two years after no. 61520 had made its final journey. The B12s were principal express engines in their day.

18.8.57

The 04 class certainly deserves a 'classic design' title. They were introduced by J.G. Robinson for the Great Central Railway in 1911. Within a short time the First World War broke out and the government chose the design for military service on the continent. Many more were constructed, and some of those in Great Central stock were also commandeered. Engines of this type were to find themselves in many distant countries. No. 63618, pictured here at March, was completed at Gorton in March 1914; it remained in service until February 1963.

13.3.55

The 'Clauds' allocated to March depot were used on local passenger and parcel trains and were maintained in good external condition. No. 62605 was one of the class rebuilt with a round-topped boiler, but still retaining the original footplating. It finished its days at March being withdrawn in June 1957. On arrival at Stratford Works it remained more or less intact for a month before being cut up.

13.5.55

J17 no. 65562 was used on several enthusiasts specials in its final years and March depot always turned out the locomotive in spotless condition. No. 65562 is seen here at Ramsey East heading the Railway Correspondence & Travel Society's 'The Fensman'; note the headboard. Here participants are seen rejoining the train (the hard way!) ready for the next stage of the tour. No. 65562 was withdrawn in August 1958.

24.7.55

J17 no. 65562 stands at Whittlesey ready to work an enthusiasts' special over the freight-only Benwick branch. Those taking part would leave the comfort of coaches and travel over the branch in open wagons. Only a comparatively small number of J17s were capable of working passenger trains, although no. 65562 was only hauling the train over the branch on this occasion. A B1 4–6–0 was the principal motive power for 'Fensman no. 2'.

9.9.56

No. 62618, one of the ex-Royal 'Clauds', this time in lined-out British Railways black livery. It makes easy work of the four-coach train on its way to Cambridge. Note the burnished ring on the smokebox door and the white disc instead of lamps.

23.5.53

The 02 class was introduced by Sir Nigel Gresley in 1918. The majority of them were built at Doncaster Works, with a batch of ten constructed in 1921 by the North British Locomotive Company. No. 63926, pictured here at March, was among the last to remain in service and was withdrawn in September 1963. This engine was one of those built by North British Locomotive Company; it received a side window cab in 1940 and was rebuilt to 02/4 specification in March 1961.

23.6.63

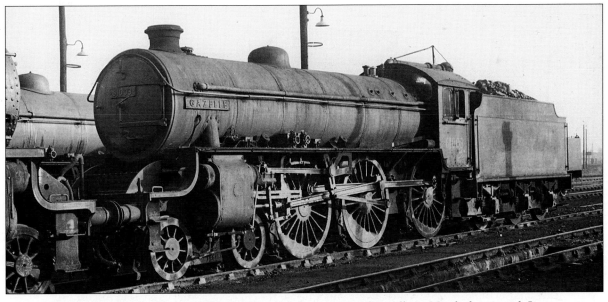

For several months B1 no. 61003 *Gazelle* was to be seen standing idle in March depot yard. It was an Immingham engine at the time, and it appears to be fully coaled, ready to return to its home depot. It was built at Darlington Works for the LNER, and completed in November 1943 as no. 8304; in 1946 it was renumbered 1003 and finally as no. 61003 in December 1948. It is not known if it ever worked again before withdrawal in December 1965.

24.1.65

When this picture of class 04/8 no. 63884 was taken at March in 1963, quite a number of Eastern Region engines were still around as there remained six months to closure. After that date steam still worked in for a considerable time, albeit with mostly London Midland Region engines. No. 63884 had an interesting history. Built in 1919 at the North British Locomotive Company's Queens Park Works for the government as ROD (Railway Operating Dept) 2126, it was purchased by the LNER in May 1927 as a class 04/3; it was rebuilt to 04/7 in 1940 and to 04/8 in October 1956 and was withdrawn in August 1962.

26.5.63

This study of 01 no. 63725 at March reveals much detail. The engine was built as an 04 in August 1919 and was rebuilt at Gorton Works in 1945. These were the standard LNER heavy goods locomotives: it was intended that 160 would be rebuilt, but in the event only 58 actually were, mainly because of the availability of the 'Austerities' after the war. An 01 was chosen for the interchange trials in 1948. During the 1950s a considerable number of the class were to be found on the Great Central with a small number in the north-east working Consett iron ore trains. No. 63725 was withdrawn in July 1965.

26.5.63

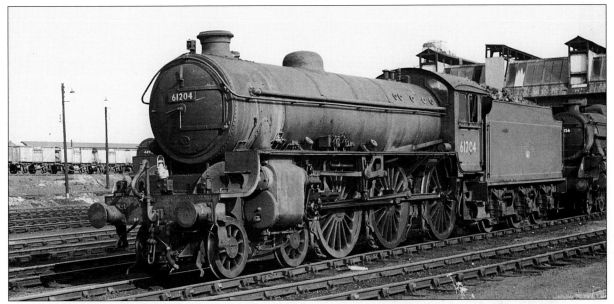

There were two separate shed buildings at March depot. B1 no. 61204 was photographed standing outside the smaller of the two, a five-road through shed. Two LMR visitors, both class 5s, were nearby. In all, 410 B1s were constructed; these were the Eastern Region's equivalent to the class 5s on the LMR. They were built at Darlington, Gorton, North British Locomotive Company and Vulcan Foundry. No. 61204 was a North British Locomotive Company engine completed in June 1947; withdrawn in November 1963, it was transferred to service stock for carriage warming.

26.5.63

Spare locomotives were sometimes used as stationary boilers at locomotive depots, supplying steam for various purposes. J17 no. 65541 was withdrawn in September 1962. It is seen here in the shed yard at March following a spell as a stationary boiler; the dome cover is lying loose and a buffer has been removed, possibly as a replacement for another engine. Pipework can also be seen where the safety valves were. Numerous bits and pieces litter the footplating. No. 65541 was in a row of engines awaiting their final journey.

26.5.63

The motive power for the majority of The Railway Correspondence & Travel Society's 'Fensman no. 2' excursions was the immaculate B1 no. 61391 of New England depot. Here, the train is reloading for the next stage of the journey. The participants had just enjoyed a trip over the freight-only Benwick branch in open goods wagons behind J17 no. 65562.

9.9.56

March, with its massive hump-shunting marshalling yards, was still a busy place in the 1950s. The locomotive depot was home to many goods engines of various types. None of the 04 class was allocated there in the 1950s although they were frequent visitors. No. 63657 was one of those built for the government, acquiring the number ROD 1618; it was bought by the LNER in 1927, remaining in service until September 1962. Note the large water tank mounted over part of the shed roof.

13.3.55

March had a large allocation of K1 class 2–6–0s. Introduced by A.H. Peppercorn in 1949, seventy new locomotives were built in all. No. 62038 is seen here at March. The prototype engine LNER 3445 *MacCallin Mor* was rebuilt from a K4 in 1945, becoming BR no. 61997, and was officially classified K1/1. It spent most of its time on the West Highland line, remaining in service until June 1961. The new constructions were a mixed traffic design, and those on the Eastern Region were mostly used on freight workings. On the difficult West Highland line, K1s were often seen on passenger trains.

13.3.55

This photograph shows clearly the K1's 5ft 2in driving wheels and the clean outline of these powerful engines, which had a tractive effort of 32,081lb. All the new locomotives were built by the North British Locomotive Company between 1949 and 1950. No. 62038 was completed in September 1949, remaining in service until October 1963. Fortunately one example of the class has survived into preservation, having been retained originally as a possible boiler for the preserved K4. Luckily the K1 was eventually restored and has been a very useful engine for many years since then.

13.3.55

The LNER handed over a great many 2–8–0 heavy goods engines to British Railways in 1948. Among them was this class 02 no. 63924, a Retford engine, pictured here at March ready for its return working. As with all Eastern Region depots, individual photography permits were not issued, and the only way in was to join an official party and try to run the gauntlet of the eagle-eyed shed foreman!

13.3.55

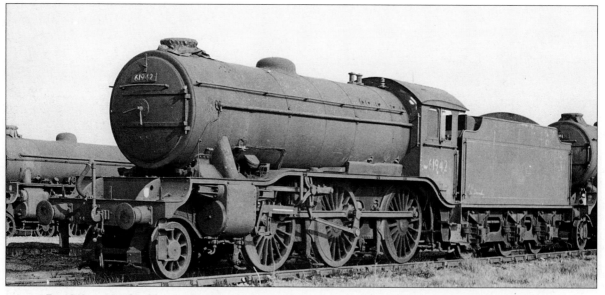

By 1963 a considerable number of stored engines were to be found in the shed yards at March, all with their chimneys covered by a piece of old tarpaulin in the traditional method. Among them were K3s, a class that had a long association with March. No. 61942 had been condemned in September 1962. Locomotives were being withdrawn in huge numbers at this time and many spent several months in storage before they were towed away for scrap.

6.5.63

Allocated the departmental number 24, B1 class no. 61323 was to see further use, following a period in store, as a stationary boiler in departmental stock. However, shortly afterwards it was condemned, in November 1963; another engine took its place, also becoming no. 24, and this one remained on these duties for three years. Low evening light highlights the running gear in this picture.

9.63

J17 class no. 65582 had been withdrawn for eight months when this picture was taken, and it was just one of many locomotives in the same position lying at March depot, all awaiting their final journey. The tender was still full of coal, which was unusual with stored engines; whether or not anyone troubled to empty it before it went to the scrapyard is anyone's guess.

23.6.63

Class 01 no. 63780 and 'Britannia' no. 70030 were both stored at March, fully coaled and their chimneys covered. The 'Britannia' was taken out of store and transferred to the London Midland Region, but no. 63780 was not so lucky, being condemned in July 1963. There were very few active steam engines allocated to March in 1963, the majority of those that remained there being mostly transferred to Staveley.

23.6.63

Most of the C12 class 4–4–2Ts ran with shorter chimneys than the one fitted to no. 67395 pictured here at March. Why the engine was there is not known, as it was allocated to the North Eastern Region at Hull Botanic Gardens shed. This engine was built at Doncaster to the design of H. A. Ivatt and was completed in July 1907. It managed almost fifty years' service before it fell victim to a cutting torch.

13.3.55

Seventeen B1s were transferred to departmental stock for carriage heating, all being given a departmental number. This was no. 23, although the engine still carried its front number plate, no. 61300. They were used as stationary boilers, and although the couplings were removed they could run under their own power to a depot for maintenance. No. 23 was condemned in November 1965.

30.8.64

The last four examples of the J20 class were withdrawn from March depot in September 1962. One of the four was no. 64699. Twenty-five of these powerful engines were built at Stratford to the design of A.J. Hill, and they were the last of a series of 0–6–0s. All were taken into British Railways stock, the class remaining intact until January 1959. In the following year, however, inroads were made into these engines.

9.9.62

The chimneys fitted to the ex-Great Central class N5 0–6–2Ts did little for their general appearance. As the standard shunting tanks of the Great Central, they were to be found at most depots. Only a handful were not taken into British Railways stock. No. 69354 was photographed at Neasden, and was one of ten allocated there at the time. The Neasden depot came under the control of the King's Cross district. No. 69354 was built by Beyer Peacock & Company in 1900 and completed sixty years' service.

20.3.55

Between 1903 and 1905, forty of these C13 class 4–4–2Ts were built to the design of J.G. Robinson for suburban services on the Great Central. All were handed over to British Railways. Three were allocated to Neasden in the mid-1950s, no. 67420 being one of them; this engine worked the Chesham branch, and also performed carriage pilot duties at Marylebone. It was withdrawn in December 1958, the same year that Neasden passed into London Midland Region control.

20.3.55

H.A. Ivatt introduced the J5 class in 1910. Twenty were built for goods workings, all at Doncaster Works. I was lucky to capture one on film: this is no. 65494 ready for the road at Colwick depot. By this time the last few survivors were mostly employed on local goods and shunting work, although it was not unusual to see them on passenger trains during the summer. Withdrawals commenced in 1953 and by the start of 1955 only one remained, no. 65494, which was condemned in January 1955.

4.4.54

The K2 class engines were officially classified as mixed traffic engines. On the Eastern Region during the 1950s they were usually to be seen on goods or parcels working and occasionally on passenger trains. On the notorious West Highland line they were widely used on the Fort William passenger services until they were generally replaced by more modern motive power. No. 61754 is pictured here at Colwick, its home shed. Withdrawals of the 75-strong class commenced in 1955 with the last survivors going in 1961; no. 61754 was withdrawn in December 1959.

4.4.54

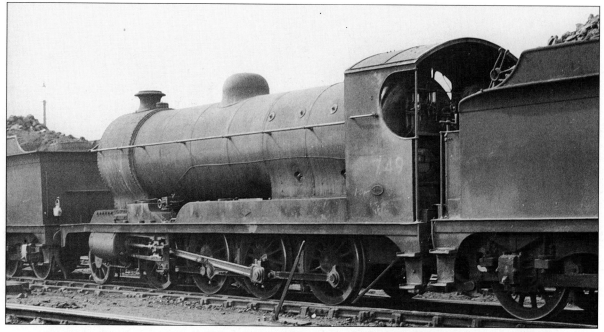

There was a considerable amount of variation among the 04 class locomotives. No. 63749 was officially classified 04/7; it was rebuilt in 1940 with a shortened 02-type boiler, at the same time retaining its Great Central-pattern smokebox. This engine was built by the North British Locomotive Company for the government for service overseas, and was taken into LNER stock in April 1928. It remained in service until October 1959. The picture was taken at Colwick.

4.4.54

Visitors to Annesley depot in the 1950s would be sure of finding a number of 01 class 2–8–0s present. These were rebuilds from the 04 class first introduced by Edward Thompson in 1944. In all fifty-eight were rebuilt: these had type 100A boilers, Walschaerts valve gear and new cylinders with 225lb boiler pressure. No. 63717 had recently received a coat of paint on the smokebox and chimney, and is seen here with two other members of the class. The Annesley 01s were widely used on freights to Woodford.

4.4.54

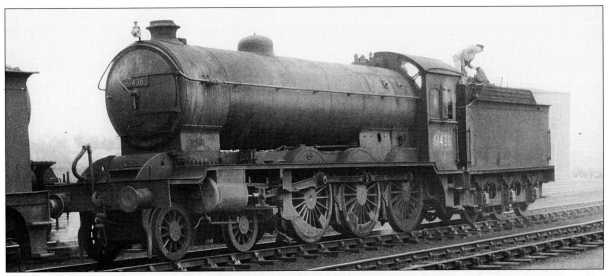

During the 1950s enthusiasts found Woodford Halse shed particularly interesting as there would almost always be one or more B16 class 4–6–0s from the North Eastern region present. Woodford was a sizeable shed, home to nearly fifty engines at the time of my visit, on a grey dismal day which did little to help smoke disperse. No. 61436 was a York engine, and the fireman appears to be sorting through coal on the tender.

27.3.55

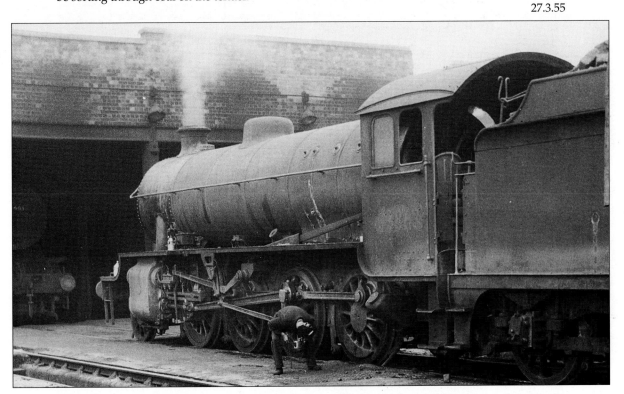

One of Woodford shed's fitters inspecting O1 no. 63863, which would appear to have brake problems. Note particularly the very grimy condition of the engine – the cab side number is barely visible. These were very powerful engines, and like others employed on heavy freight work they rarely, if ever, received attention from cleaners between works visits.

27.3.55

Another York B16 comes on to Woodford Halse shed at the end of its journey. No. 61430 was built at Darlington Works for the North Eastern Railway in 1921. York B16s travelled far and wide, even working on the East Coast main line south of Peterborough on rare occasions. York had a sizeable allocation of well over thirty engines. In the summer months they could often be seen hauling excursion trains.

27.3.55

Lincoln St Marks was a subshed of the Lincoln depot and did not have its own allocation. J39 class no. 64714 was photographed in the shed yard on a Sunday morning. During the 1950s you would be most likely to find J39s and, if you were lucky, D11 'Directors' at St Marks, as well as the ex-Midland Railway 0–6–0T no. 41686.

14.8.55

One of Lincoln depot's J39s takes water at St Marks shed. The J39 class consisted of 289 engines, although not all were to be found in the Eastern Region. Introduced by Sir Nigel Gresley in 1926, they were powerful engines with 5ft 2in driving wheels and 25,665lb tractive effort, making them at home on all but the heaviest goods workings and also at times on passenger workings.

14.8.55

Lincoln depot was of Great Northern origin but also had a number of ex-Great Central engines in its allocation including N5 0–6–2Ts for shunting duties. No. 69275 was one of these. It is seen here in company with a B1 class 4–6–0 and WD no. 90522. Lincoln, shed code 40A, was home to around seventy-five engines during the 1950s.

14.8.55

There were two sheds at Retford – one of Great Northern origin, the other of Great Central – about 700 yards apart. In the mid-1950s they both came under the shedcode 36E, with a total allocation of seventy locomotives. J6 no. 64245 is seen here in the GN depot yard.

25.8.57

D11 'Director' class no. 62666 *Zeebrugge* waiting at Lincoln St Marks station before commencing its cross-country run. Four of these locomotives were allocated to Lincoln in the 1950s including the sole survivor, no. 62660 *Butler Henderson*, now part of the National Collection and currently at York Railway Museum.

14.8.55

The 02 class had three-cylinder engines as opposed to the 01s and 04s which had two. All three classes had 4ft 8in driving wheels. In their later years they are best remembered for the Highdyke iron ore trains over the difficult single-line branch. Grantham depot had a sizeable stud of these which not only worked on the branch but also hauled block trains to two destinations in the north of England. Other members of the class worked on heavy goods traffic. No. 63945 was a Retford engine when photographed at Lincoln.

25.8.57

Summer weekends were busy times at Skegness in the 1950s. At that time many people still travelled by rail for their holidays. Excursions were organised from numerous points, and this resulted in the station having several trains ready for departure in the early evening. K2 no. 61745, a Boston locomotive, is pictured heading a service train.

19.6.55

Another picture taken at Skegness on a dull summer Sunday. B12 no. 61553 heads an excursion train ready for its return journey. Once a month during the summer an excursion ran from King's Cross to Skegness, picking up at many stations on the East Coast main line. The return fare in 1955 from Huntingdon to Skegness was 9s 3d, leaving at 9.55 a.m. and arriving at the resort at 12.08.

19.6.55

Lincoln depot also had a number of ex-Great Eastern 0–6–0Ts. These useful engines were scattered far and wide in LNER days; you could find them even in the north of Scotland. No. 68553 was a J69/1, introduced in 1902; this particular example was built at Stratford in 1895 as a J67, and rebuilt to J69 in 1906. They were distinctive engines with their tall chimneys. No. 68553 was withdrawn in December 1958.

14.8.55

Engines under repair were a common sight at many depots. Often they would be moved outside to await the return of re-metalled bearings after running hot; this was possibly the case with J39 no. 64937 at Lincoln depot. Numerous parts can be seen lying on the footplating. In the background is J69 no. 68605.

25.8.57

Some depots were very untidy. This is Lincoln, and doubtless the rail chairs, oil can, ladders, firebars and miscellaneous junk would have presented hazards to enginemen in the dark. K3 no. 61961 was a visitor from Doncaster shed. Just visible on the smokebox door is a chalked reporting number; evidently, the engine had worked a special or excursion previously.

25.8.57

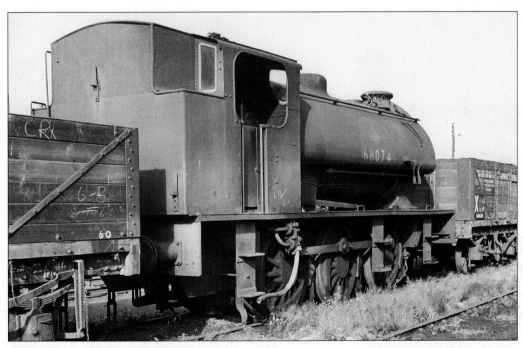

In 1946 the LNER purchased seventy-five of these 'Austerity' 0–6–0STs from the Ministry of Supply. These engines had been built by six different private companies but were all classified J94. A considerable number were allocated to Eastern Region depots. No. 68074 was surplus to requirements at Immingham and had been placed in store. This engine was built by Andrew Barclay & Company in 1945. It was eventually returned to traffic and withdrawn in October 1962.

25.8.57

The thirteen Q1 class 0–8–0Ts were rebuilt from Q4 class 0–8–0s by Edward Thompson; they were designed for heavy shunting work and the first Q1 appeared in 1942. They were found in several parts of the LNER. No. 69934 is seen here at Frodingham; seven of the class were allocated there at the time this picture was taken. Withdrawals commenced in 1954 with the last few, including no. 69934, going in 1959.

25.8.57

The C14 class 4–4–2Ts were introduced by J.G. Robinson for the Great Central Railway in 1903. In all forty were built, principally for working suburban and branch-line trains. All the class were still in service and taken over by British Railways. In the early 1950s withdrawals commenced and by 1959 all had fallen victim to the cutter's torch. No. 67434 had just over a year left when this picture was taken.

24.6.56

Two ex-Great Central Railway tank locomotives pictured at Mexborough. This was a sizeable depot with over 100 engines in the 1950s; the majority were heavy goods engines used for handling coal traffic in the area. By far the largest class was the WD 2–8–0s with well over fifty on the depot's books. N5 0–6–2T no. 69305 was one of four to be found at the shed.

24.6.56

The 04 class provided a great many years of service. The decision by the LNER to purchase a number of these fine engines to supplement those they already had when they became surplus to requirements after the First World War must have been welcomed by those involved with motive power. No. 63730 was placed in service in April 1924 and not withdrawn until January 1966.

24.6.56

An 04 in good external condition – very different to how they normally appeared in the 1950s. No. 63779, pictured at Mexborough, was one of those supplied new to the government in 1918 and allocated the number ROD 1875; it was placed in traffic by the LNER in July 1927 and remained in service until April 1962, well repaying its purchase price.

24.6.56

In 1945 the rebuilt Gresley A10 class 'Pacific' *Great Northern* emerged from Doncaster Works to the design of Edward Thompson; the engine was now classified A1/1. The rebuilding involved new frames and many other components, and very little of the original engine remained. This was the forerunner of the A1s introduced in 1948. In the intervening period A.H. Peppercorn had taken over the reins, and this resulted in a number of changes. No. 60113 *Great Northern* was allocated to Doncaster depot, where this picture was taken, for its last five years..It was withdrawn in December 1962.

25.8.57

During the 1950s a trip to Doncaster was something to look forward to. Would any of those elusive Gresley 'Pacifics' from north of the border or the north of England be on shed, either fresh from or awaiting works? A3 no. 60036 *Colombo* was a typical example, having just been coaled and watered ready for running-in trials. This engine was allocated to Leeds Neville Hill depot. It would almost certainly have had at least one more works visit before withdrawal in November 1964.

10.11.57

Bright as a new pin, this is K1 class no. 62049, having just received a general overhaul at Doncaster Works. It is seen here on shed ready for running-in trials before returning to its home depot, York. The K1s were very useful mixed traffic engines, and examples of this class were transferred to York depot from the mid-1950s onwards.

10.11.57

The 6ft diameter boiler fitted to the K3 class 2–6–0s can be clearly seen in this photograph of no. 61980, pictured here at its home shed, Annesley. K3s were classified as a mixed traffic design, their 30,130lb tractive effort made them capable of handling heavy goods. Among their duties were fast goods, especially parcels, livestock and perishable traffic. They were often to be seen on passenger services in the early 1950s, with the summer months seeing them in use on excursion trains.

4.4.54

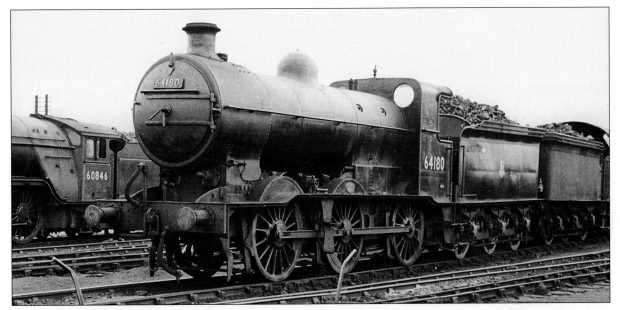

Working out how many times J6 no. 64180 had been overhauled at Doncaster Works since it left there in 1911 would require a considerable amount of research! This picture was taken as it was ready to return to its home shed, Boston, after what was almost certainly its last 'general' as it was withdrawn in March 1960. Two years later the last of the class made its final journey.

23.9.56

This ex-North Eastern Railway G5 class 0–4–4T no. 67269 was an unusual sight at Doncaster. It was en route to Darlington for scrapping. This engine was one of three allocated to Cambridge to work the Bartlow branch; all were push-pull fitted. It was built at Darlington Works in 1896 and completed sixty years' service.

23.9.56

King's Cross depot B1 no. 61200 had just been through Doncaster Works for a general overhaul and is pictured on the shed, running-in trials finished, ready for the return journey. No. 61200 was completed by the North British Locomotive Company in June 1947 and withdrawn in December 1962. The duties once worked by these engines had been taken over by diesel power.

23.9.56

Many depots had what was known as a 'cripple siding', where engines that had failed or needed attention would be left out of the way until such time as fitters could get to them. J6 class no. 64179, an 0–6–0, was a Doncaster engine; it presented a strange sight as the rear pair of drive wheels had been removed while the axle boxes were re-metalled.

23.9.56

The last batch of J50 class 0–6–0Ts were completed at Gorton Works in 1938–9 and fitted with hopper-type larger bunkers. No. 68980 was one of these, completed in December 1938. The J50s were powerful shunting engines and were to be found over a wide area including London. In the early 1950s you would see at least two or three before arriving at King's Cross.

23.9.56

This engine, A3 no. 60043 *Brown Jack*, caused considerable interest among number collectors at the time of my visit to Doncaster Works. It was one of several allocated to Haymarket depot, Edinburgh. A3s from that shed seldom came south of Doncaster. No. 60043 was awaiting entry into the works for a general overhaul.

23.9.56

Ardsley shed, formerly 37A, became part of the North Eastern Region in 1956, taking the shed code 56B. Class V2 2–6–2 no. 60846 was already carrying the new shed code as it stood at Doncaster shed awaiting return to the works for a general overhaul. This engine was later to be allocated to several other sheds including St Margarets, Edinburgh, where it ended its days in November 1965.

23.9.56

The J52 0–6–0STs were once commonplace in the Eastern Region, quietly going about their business in shunting yards. No. 68882 was in poor external condition when photographed under repair at Doncaster. Part of the coupling rods have been removed, and can be seen lying on the footplate. Despite the problems this engine remained in service until January 1958.

23 9.56

Anyone living near Doncaster regularly had the opportunity of photographing ex-works engines. J6 no. 64267 was resplendent, freshly painted after what was to be its last general overhaul. Even the Great Northern brass works plate over the centre driving wheel had been burnished. But time was running out rapidly for the engine: it was condemned in July 1958.

23.9.56

In the mid-1950s J6 class 0–6–0s were still receiving general overhauls although odd examples had already been withdrawn. No. 64256 was a Colwick engine, pictured here at Doncaster shed fresh from overhaul. As with several others ex-works at this time, this would have been this locomotive's last 'general'; it was withdrawn in April 1960.

23.9.56

Engines from the North Eastern and Scottish Region line up at Doncaster. On the right is A3 no. 60037 *Hyperion* of Haymarket. A1 no. 60155 *Borderer* was a Gateshead engine and the V2 in the background, no. 60976, was a York engine.

24.6.56

The decision to purchase seventy-five 'Riddles', Ministry of Supply 0–6–0STs, was a good move as these powerful engines were to give many years of service. No. 68020 was built by W.G. Bagnall and Company in September 1944 and remained in service until June 1962.

24.6.56

The Immingham depot K3s were frequently used on fast fish trains to London and elsewhere. No. 61838, seen here fresh from a general overhaul at Doncaster Works, was one of the batch of twelve allocated to the depot in the mid-1950s. In due course B1s took over many of the duties previously worked by this class. No. 61838 remained in service until March 1960.

24.6.56

York B16s travelled far and wide, so Doncaster was a comparatively local run for no. 61472. These very useful mixed traffic locomotives were introduced by Sir Vincent Raven for the North Eastern Railway in 1920. No. 61472 was rebuilt in 1945 as a B16/3 with Walschaerts valve gear. It was withdrawn in April 1964 after forty-five years' service.

24.6.56

There was a certain amount of variation to be found among the 04s. No. 63615 was rebuilt in December 1939 as 04/7; this involved the addition of a 02-type boiler, but retaining the Great Central smokebox. No. 63615 was completed at Gorton Works in February 1914 and had a long service life, being withdrawn in September 1964. The engine is seen here at a smoky Mexborough shed.

24.6.56

This is a typical 04 class 2–8–0. No. 63665 was built by Kitson & Company in September 1918 for the Railway Operating Department and was later sold to the LNER. These engines were fitted with steam brakes only and no water scoop. Most of their work was on heavy mineral trains, especially near collieries. No. 63665 was photographed at Tuxford. This engine remained in service until December 1963.

25.8.57

Fifty-eight class 04 locomotives were rebuilt between 1944 and 1947 to a design by E. Thompson. They had a type 100A boiler, Walschaerts valve gear and new cylinders. No. 63760 was in good external condition and had undergone a general overhaul not long before. This engine was rebuilt in August 1946, twenty-eight years after it first entered service in November 1962.

25.8.57

The 01 class engines were rebuilds of 04s by E. Thompson and they first appeared in 1944. No. 63872 was rebuilt in May 1946. Typical of many steam locomotives at this time, it was covered in soot and grime. On the front of the tender is a chalked inscription: 'floor boards missing', presumably from an earlier repair, as it had been made ready for the road.

9.63

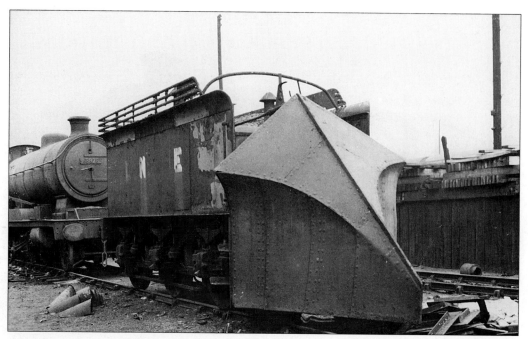

After the engines to which they were coupled were withdrawn from service, many old locomotive tenders were given a second lease of life, being used as snowploughs, sludge- and water-carriers. This example had been numbered into a departmental series as no. 951580; it also carried the number (395), possibly the original tender number. It was photographed at Mexborough shed. Close examination reveals some sort of ballast clinging to the far side.

24.6.56

In January 1955, the year before this picture was taken at Mexborough shed, no. 63628 had been rebuilt to class 04/8. This was its second rebuild in a long history that started at Gorton Works in 1919. Its original number was ROD 2007. It was taken into Great Central stock in the June of the same year. Its first rebuild was to 04/5 specification in 1932; the 04/8s were rebuilt with B1-type boilers but retained their original cylinders. No. 63628 was among the last survivors, being condemned in September 1965.

24.6.56

This picture shows the larger tender fitted to the 04s. No. 63779 was photographed at Mexborough, its tender piled high ready for an early start on the Monday morning. This was one of the ex-ROD engines fitted with steam brakes only and no water scoop. It was to remain in service until April 1962.

24.6.56

The thirteen examples of the Q1 class 0–8–0Ts were rebuilt by E. Thompson from Q4 class locomotives between 1942 and 1945 for heavy shunting work but the class did not last long. Withdrawals commenced in 1954 and by 1959 all had made their final journey to the scrap yard. No. 69934 was photographed at Mexborough surrounded by 2–8–0s; this engine was among those which went in 1959.

24.6.56

An N5 0–6–2T on shed pilot duties at Barnsley, getting engines into the right order for Monday morning. It has just towed three 2–8–0s out of the shed including no. 63718, recently rebuilt to class 04/8. This engine was originally built by Robert Stephenson & Company in 1919, and it managed forty-three years' service.

24.6.56

Sunday was a good day to catch engines at their home shed, especially the heavy goods types which would be away early on the Monday morning. Class 04 no. 63727 was photographed outside its home depot, Barnsley. This one was built for the Great Central in 1912 by Kitson and Company. It had both steam and vacuum brakes and a water scoop, unlike the ROD engines.

24.6.56

In all 174 engines of the very useful J11 class were taken into British Railways stock. They were built at Gorton Works and also by Neilson, Reed & Company, Beyer Peacock & Company, the Vulcan Foundry and the Yorkshire Engine Company between 1901 and 1910. They were commonly referred to as 'Pom-Poms', a nickname derived from a quick-firing gun in use in the South African war because the locomotive's sharp exhaust sounded rather similar. No. 64425, pictured at Barnsley, was built at Gorton in 1907 and completed fifty-three years' service.

24.6.56

The shunter in charge of locomotive movements takes a few minutes to chat to a duty fitter at Barnsley shed. Class 04/8 no. 63704 had been rebuilt in December 1953. This engine was one of the 04s built in 1918 for the government. It was taken into LNER stock in 1928 and scrapped in March 1963.

24.6.56

Bright as a new pin, this is J11 no. 64365 at Sheffield Darnall shed having recently undergone a general overhaul. This would certainly have been its last as the engine was withdrawn in August 1959. While their principal work was goods traffic they were not unknown on passenger trains.

24.6.56

I was to photograph A3 no. 60050 *Persimmon* on several occasions, especially in its final years when it was allocated to New England. When this picture was taken at Sheffield Darnall it was among those working on the Great Central and allocated to Neasden depot.

24.6.56

British Railways took over 174 members of the Robinson J11 class; these had been built at Gorton Works by four private companies. The J11s were useful, powerful locomotives, and some examples were fitted with slide and piston valves. The last member of the class was withdrawn in 1962. No. 64365 was photographed art Lincoln in a typical work-stained condition; it was to soldier on for another four years before withdrawal.

14.8.55

During the mid-1950s Sheffield Darnall was a sizeable depot with over 100 engines in its allocation, including a number of 2–8–0s. Class 04 no. 63695 was one of those, seen here outside its home shed. This engine was typical of the large number purchased by the LNER; it went into service in September 1925.

24.6.56

In the 1960s many private scrapyards cut up locomotives, but before this scrapping was done at the locomotive works. Engines were often towed considerable distances to these private scrapyards. A few Eastern Region engines ended their days at Cohens of Kettering. No. 61406 was allocated to Immingham depot for some years.

21.8.66

B1 no. 61360 had been towed to Cohens of Kettering with its valve gear and coupling rods partly dismantled. Within a short time it would have been reduced to a pile of scrap metal.

21.8.66

Retford depot had a large number of 0–6–0s in its allocation, including several J11s of the type seen here. No. 64403 was a visitor at the Great Central depot; the other 0–6–0s were J6s and J39s. Also based at Retford depot were a considerable number of 04 class 2–8–0s, which were joined in the late 1950s by 02 class engines. The six B1 class 4–6–0s at the depot were mostly used on passenger and fast goods trains.

25.8.57

The first semi-fast from King's Cross on a Sunday morning consisted of four coaches and was usually worked by a 'Pacific'. Here, class A1 no. 60136 *Alcazar* awaits the 'right away' at Huntingdon. Note the close-coupled suburban set in the background, also the water crane and stove, once a very familiar sight on the railways. No examples of the class made it into preservation; however, no. 60163 *Tornado* is, at the time of writing, under construction.

3.8.52